TRUE
RINGS
THE
HEART

TRUE RINGS THE HEART

SUSAN DEAN SMALLWOOD

Deseret Book Company
Salt Lake City, Utah

To Paulette, my sister for eternity

Library of Congress Cataloging-in-Publication Data

Smallwood, Susan Dean.
    True rings the heart / by Susan Dean Smallwood.
       p. cm.
    ISBN 0-87579-355-X (hardbound)
    I. Title.
PS3569.M345T74   1990
813'.54—dc20   90-38526
                                                CIP

Printed in the United States of America

10   9   8   7   6   5   4   3   2   1

1

"You look beautiful in red," Paul Danforth whispered into Elizabeth's ear. They hesitated inside the wide French doors of the country club ballroom. As Elizabeth reached up to touch Paul's cheek and smile a thank you at him, the lights of the brilliant chandelier hanging from the center of the ceiling twinkled off the diamond bracelet Elizabeth was wearing. She did feel beautiful.

The party was the first real one they had been to since Megan had been born six months earlier, and Elizabeth felt ready for it. The band was playing slow and romantic dance music, just the kind they liked, and the food spread over the tables looked inviting and smelled delicious. And it appeared as if Ben, the boss, had the champagne flowing as freely as he usually did.

Elizabeth was always excited about coming to the club. Belonging to it was one of the perks that came with being a partner in the law firm. When Paul had joined the firm two years before, Elizabeth had been most excited about the club membership. She enjoyed the tennis and the pool, of course, and even the beauty of the grounds and mansion.

But for her, who had never really belonged to anything or anyone her whole life, what she enjoyed most was the belonging.

Paul pointed across the room. "There's Ben. I need to talk to him about a case that came in today."

"Paul," Elizabeth said. "This is a party — you're not supposed to talk business."

"It's a business party," he said. "Give me five minutes to straighten out a problem, and I promise I won't leave your side the rest of the evening. A deal?"

"I guess so. I'll head for the champagne."

"Somehow I knew you would." He smiled before walking away.

A waiter deftly filled her stemmed glass from one of the streams of champagne cascading down the three-tiered fountain and handed the glass to her. She took her first sip and turned to find Carla, the boss's wife, beside her. Not everyone could relax around Carla, but Elizabeth had always done better than most.

"Hi, Carla," she said. "Your dress is gorgeous. From your dress shop, of course?"

"Of course," Carla said. She swept her own glass under the fountain. "Your dress is beautiful, too. Thank goodness you kept your figure after the baby."

"Thank goodness for exercise videos," Elizabeth said. She hadn't really been sure until that morning that she would be able to zip her dress up again.

"So, are you tired of dirty diapers yet and ready to enter the real-estate market again?"

Elizabeth laughed. "Sorry, but I'm still enjoying motherhood. However, I did talk to my ex-boss this morning. I told him that I'd handle some rental business for him a couple of afternoons a week. He's a little short-handed, and the work will keep me in touch with the real-estate business in case I ever want to go back full-time."

"Speaking of motherhood . . . " She rolled her eyes toward a nearby couple, dropping her voice to a whisper. "Have you gotten to know the Robertsons yet? They have five children. Can you believe it?"

Elizabeth watched as the Robertsons sat down at a small table. She hadn't really gotten to know them very well since the husband—she couldn't remember his name—had just joined the firm several weeks ago. Maybe tonight would be a good night.

As good as his promise, Paul was back at her side, accepting a glass from the waiter and exchanging first hellos, then good-byes with Carla as someone else pulled her away.

"Honey," Elizabeth suggested, "why don't we go over and sit by the Robertsons for a little while? I don't really know them yet. Do you?"

"I've played handball a couple of lunchtimes with Nephi," Paul said. "He always beats me."

They started over to the table. "What's his name again?" Elizabeth asked in a whisper.

"Nephi," he said. "They're from Salt Lake City. It's a Mormon name or something. They're real involved in the Mormon church."

She hesitated beyond earshot of their table. "You never told me that."

He put his hand under her elbow and started her walking again. "Bets, sweetheart," he said. "I knew you wouldn't be interested."

"You're right."

When they reached the table, Nephi stood to shake Paul's hand. He was as tall as Paul but slender and blond.

"Paul," Nephi said, "have you met my wife, Jeanine?"

"Once, I think," Paul answered. "And this is my wife, Bets."

"Elizabeth," Elizabeth corrected him. "Paul's the only one I let call me Bets, and sometimes I wonder about that."

"Okay," Paul said. He pulled out the chair next to Jeanine for his wife as Jeanine smiled over at her.

"I should apologize for not having welcomed you to the area sooner," Elizabeth said. "But I'm barely getting organized again since my baby was born."

"How old is your baby?" Jeanine asked. "Little boy or girl?"

"A little girl—Megan. She's six months old."

"I have Sarah," Jeanine said. "She's almost eight months old."

"Someone told me you have five children," Elizabeth said. "Is that true?"

"It sure is," Nephi said. "It seems more like twenty some nights."

Elizabeth looked at Jeanine admiringly. "You don't look like you have five children."

"Thanks," Jeanine said. "I hear that a lot, but I don't really know what a mother of five children should look like."

"Tired, I guess," Elizabeth said. "Not little and pretty like you are."

Jeanine blushed. "Thank you. But I do get awfully tired sometimes."

A waiter reached between them to replace Elizabeth's empty glass with a full one, but Jeanine refused his offer to her and instead requested a ginger ale. As Paul and Elizabeth exchanged a glance, Nephi asked for one also. Elizabeth hadn't realized Ben hired anyone who wouldn't drink at a party.

Nephi and Paul slipped easily into a conversation about a current case, which left Elizabeth sipping her champagne and wondering what in the world she could talk to Jeanine about now. But Jeanine began first.

"Do you work outside your home?" she asked Elizabeth.

"I'm a realtor," Elizabeth answered. "But I haven't

worked since the baby was born. I'm going to start working a couple of afternoons a week during Megan's naptime, but that's all I'm interested in. Do you work?"

"No. I was going to law school part-time before we left Salt Lake, but we moved here too late to apply for the fall semester at UVA, so I guess I'll take a semester off."

Elizabeth was impressed. "How do you go to law school and manage all those children?"

"Sometimes, I wonder," Jeanine said, laughing. "I think I'll be glad to have some time off. Maybe we can take the babies to the park one morning before it gets too cold."

"That sounds great," Elizabeth said.

As the waiter brought the glasses of ginger ale, Elizabeth caught part of Nephi's and Paul's conversation. It was something about some temple. Her glance and smile toward them must have indicated an interest she didn't actually feel because Paul turned to her and grabbed her hand.

"Bets," he said, "do you remember that beautiful white church we saw off the Beltway in Washington, D.C.? That's a Mormon temple."

"How interesting," Elizabeth said. She blotted her lips with a napkin.

"Maybe you all can go to church there one Sunday," Paul said. "It's only a couple of hours away."

"Well, actually," Nephi said, "we don't hold church services there. In fact, the temples are closed on Sunday."

"Hmmm," Paul said. "What are they for then?"

"Marriages, for one thing," Nephi said. "We believe that when you're married in the temple, your marriage is for eternity, not just 'till death do you part.'"

Paul leaned forward on the table, obviously interested in what Nephi was saying. Elizabeth, though, was ready for the conversation to end. He knew there was no part for her in any conversation about religion, but evidently his interest was stronger than his usual consideration for her.

She loved him dearly, but she wished he'd be content being the Catholic he'd been all his life and stop searching for something he hadn't even been able to define to himself. As she blocked Paul's response from her mind and looked around the room, concentrating on the rise and fall of voices and the music, she realized the band was playing one of her favorite songs from their college days.

She turned to Jeanine, who was listening intently to her husband explaining something to Paul. "Don't you just love that song?" Elizabeth said. "It reminds me of being in college."

"It's one of my favorites." Jeanine smiled.

"Honey." Elizabeth pulled on Paul's arm. "Let's dance before that song ends. It's one of our songs."

Paul turned reluctantly from Nephi. "Sure, sweetheart," he said. "We did come to party, didn't we?" He stood up, then helped Elizabeth to her feet. "Come on, Nephi. Maybe I can show you up on the dance floor since I can't on the handball court."

Jeanine was dragging Nephi up from the table. "You probably can," he answered Paul.

Dancing comfortably and close in Paul's arms, Elizabeth closed her eyes dreamily, thinking about the times they had danced to the same song and not about Paul's interest in the Robertsons' church. But his comment brought her back.

"Did I tell you why Nephi and Jeanine moved here?" he asked.

"Don't think so," she answered. She waved at another couple over Paul's shoulder. "I thought you all hired him."

"We did, but they wanted to move to Virginia because he was a missionary for their church here in Waynesboro several years ago. He loved it so much that, when they saw our ad in the paper, they decided to move back. Isn't that interesting?"

"Very interesting, Paul." She nestled closer to him. "But can't we enjoy the music and forget about the Mennonites?"

"Mormons, Bets."

"Whatever."

Four or five songs and dances later, Paul and Elizabeth wove their way back to the table where Nephi and Jeanine had been for a while. "Don't like to dance much, Nephi?" Paul asked.

"In small doses," he answered. "I can't bruise Jeanine's feet too badly at one time. Besides, I need to save my strength for beating you at handball."

Elizabeth picked up a napkin and began to fan herself as they laughed.

"That's a beautiful chain you're wearing," Jeanine said to Elizabeth. She leaned over to look closer. "Is that your baby ring on it?"

Elizabeth smiled softly and held the ring out for Jeanine to see. "It was my mother's. It's the only thing I have of hers. I wear it all the time."

"It's lovely," Jeanine said. "I've given up wearing good jewelry until my youngest starts college. The babies are always breaking it."

"I know. Megan has been grabbing at my necklace a lot." She fingered the tiny ring. "I think I might put it up for a while. I couldn't stand to lose it."

Paul reached over to put his hand gently on Elizabeth's arm. "It might be best to put it up for a little, Bets."

Saying nothing more, but with her fingers still on the ring, Elizabeth turned back to Jeanine. "Let's get something to eat. Dancing makes me hungry."

She wasn't really hungry, but at least it changed the subject. Unless she was talking with Paul, she never lingered in conversations about her ring. Especially talk about taking it from around her neck.

As she followed Paul to the refreshment table, she wondered how she would feel without her ring. When she was a little girl, it had hung on a grubby string around her neck. In her teens and early twenties, it had gone through a variety of cheap chains, until Paul had given her the beautiful gold herringbone chain she now wore. The ring had connected her to a mother she had never known, a love she had never felt. But the thought of Megan breaking the chain and of the ring being lost was more unbearable than the loneliness she would feel without it.

She decided as she picked up a plate that, as soon as they got home, she would tuck her ring safely away in her jewelry box. Just for a while. Just until Megan knew what no-no meant. Paul would probably be happy about it, too. He would view it as a sign of progress on her part.

Paul whispered over her shoulder, "Having a good time, Bets?"

"I'm having a wonderful time, honey." The mood of the party, the sound of voices and music around them, and new friends blended with the closeness of the handsome husband beside her to give her the sense of security she always wanted but never seemed to hold on to. Maybe at last the feeling would stay, though. She smiled at Paul, reaching to help him in his fight with a cheese ball. Yes. Maybe at last life would be just what she wanted it to be.

CHAPTER

2

In the dim light of the bedroom, Jesselene Manning rose from her morning prayers and sat down on the edge of the bed. At five-foot-three, she could never decide if she was three inches too short for her weight or fifteen pounds too heavy for her height. Her closely cut hair was almost totally grey, and her kind, dark eyes were framed by laugh wrinkles.

Her husband, Rowland, still snored in his side of the bed. Every morning before she woke him, for as many years as she could remember, she had knelt quietly by the side of their bed to begin her day in prayer, then picked up the notepad that lay beside the clock radio and listed all she needed to accomplish that day.

This day on the top of her list, she wrote "office." She had written that on the top of her list for the last two weeks, and today was the day she was going to sign the lease on it.

Less important tasks like going to the dry cleaners and straightening up her food supply made it farther down the list. Her checklist done, she reached over to her husband and shook his shoulder. "Rowland, it's seven. Time to get up." He wiggled his toes a little, which signaled his first stage of consciousness. His second stage usually didn't occur until he smelled bacon frying and she yelled up the stairs at him again to get up.

"Mom, Mom!" her sixteen-year-old son Steve called from down the hall. "Could you sew a button on my blue shirt?"

"Sure, hon'," she called back. "Do you have the button?"

"No, it just fell off, and I can't find it. Can you find it too?"

She walked into the mess he called a room. "Yes, dear." She shook her head and kicked a few clothes around. "You're going to be the only missionary who has to take his mother on his mission with him just to get him dressed in the morning."

"That Elder Wigginson was a real slob too. Remember him?"

Jesselene just rolled her eyes. "Give me your shirt and point me to the pile where the button might have landed."

He jerked the blue shirt off his shoulder and threw it over to her. "Thanks, Mom. I've got to go blow-dry my hair. I'll help you when I'm finished if you still haven't found it."

Jesselene found the button right on top of the designated pile. She firmly believed that her children's love for her throughout the years was based on her ability to find whatever they had lost.

The delicious smell of frying bacon reached her just as she finished sewing the button. She broke the thread off with her teeth. Diane must have started breakfast, she thought. What would she do when Diane left? Jesselene had been so happy when Diane had decided to stay in town for her first two years of college and then transfer to BYU. By that time it would almost be time for Steve to leave on his mission, and the house would be so empty. Oh well, she sighed to herself, maybe she would just go on his mission with him. She didn't know how he'd ever manage without her.

Steve breezed back into the room, hair neatly blown, combed, and sprayed. "Is my shirt ready, Mom?"

"Right here," she said, handing it to him. "I've got to go help Diane with breakfast." She got up and kicked her way back through the room. "Get these clothes in the clothes basket. This morning."

"I will, Mom. I promise. If," he said with the wide grin she loved so much, "you'll get the knot out of my shoelaces. It's a real monster."

Within half an hour, all four were gathered around the kitchen table eating breakfast.

"Will you pick up my suit at the cleaners, dear?" Rowland asked.

"It's on my list," Jesselene assured him.

"Dad, you could pick up your own suit at the cleaners," Diane said lightly. "Mom is not a slave whose destiny is to do all the little things in life her family doesn't want to bother with."

Rowland put down his fork and looked seriously around the table at his family. "Don't tell me I'm a male chauvinist again today."

"I'll pick up your suit," Jesselene said. "I have to go right by there anyway. Besides, you are a male chauvinist practically every day."

"Have you decided on a name for your organization yet, Mom?" Diane asked.

"Almost," she answered. "We'll decide for sure at next Tuesday's meeting. I think it's going to be TLC, Inc. You know—tender loving care."

"Sounds great, Mom," Steve said. He moved away from the table and picked up his books off the counter. "Say, have you seen a permission slip for a field trip? You were supposed to sign it, but I sort of lost it."

"The slip's on the bulletin board, all signed," his mother said.

"Stevie, you need to learn responsibility for yourself," Diane said. "Mom won't always be around to take care of you. And take your own dishes off the table. I'm not a maid."

"You're not taking another of those Women-of-the-90s classes again this semester, are you?" Rowland asked Diane.

"No."

"Great," he said.

"Thank goodness," Steve added. "And don't call me Stevie anymore. I'm Steve."

"Sure, baby brother."

Steve kissed Jesselene on the cheek, then slapped his dad on the back. "Got to leave. I'm going where the girls appreciate me."

"Bye, hon'," Jesselene said. "Don't forget your Spanish club meeting after school."

"Mom," Diane said, "you're doing it again."

Jesselene stood and began to clear the dishes off the table. "Did you study for your sociology quiz, Diane?"

"Oh no," she said with a stricken look on her face. "Is this Friday?"

"Sure is," Rowland said. Then he put his hand over hers and teased her. "My, my, we need to learn some responsibility perhaps."

"Daddy!" She got up from the table to put her arms around her mother. "Mom, I'll clean up the kitchen tonight if you'll do it this morning while I study."

"Go on," Jesselene said. "It's almost done." It wasn't really, but she still had plenty of time. "I'll be so glad to sign the lease on this office and be open for business. I get almost frantic thinking about the women we could be helping right now."

"I know, dear," her husband said gently. He looked over at her, then pushed his chair back and held his arms out. "Come here."

Jesselene curled up on his lap as he circled her with his arms. "I'm not getting depressed," she said.

"Good, I don't want you to." He gave her a squeeze. "All you can do is the best you can, and faith will take care of the rest."

"I know, I know," she said, getting up again. Wiping away one stray little tear, she picked up more dishes. "Don't worry about me."

"I can't promise that," he said. "I love you too much." He stood up and looked down beside his chair, then under the table.

"In the hall by the front door," she said.

"What?"

"Your briefcase."

"Thanks." He planted a kiss on her cheek and messed up her hair a little. "See you tonight. Love you."

With the kitchen to herself, Jesselene sat back down with the newspaper. She couldn't fool Rowland. He knew why she was working so hard to help women and girls who needed help and love during their pregnancies. He never said anything about it, but she knew he had figured it out. Probably even before she'd admitted it to herself.

Oh Jess, she thought, slapping the newspaper closed. The Lord forgave you so long ago. When will you forgive yourself?

● ● ●

Party weekend over, Elizabeth walked Paul out to his red Mercedes Monday morning. Megan was perched on Elizabeth's hip and had a blanket wrapped around her against the slight chill of autumn. The first fallen leaves softened the couple's footsteps as they walked down the driveway.

"So what's on your agenda for the day?" Paul asked, opening the car door. He tossed his briefcase inside, then held out his hands to Megan. "Give Daddy a kiss."

"Now think, Paul," Elizabeth said. "I told you what I was doing today."

"You did?"

"I have an appointment with a woman this afternoon to sign a lease on that office space. I think her name is Jesselene Manning or Menning or something."

"Now I remember." He squeezed Megan one more time and handed her back to Elizabeth. "You won't be away from Megan long, will you?"

"Paul," she said. "You told me you didn't mind if I worked a couple of afternoons a week. Megan loves Gladys — she won't even miss me."

"Impossible," he said. Cupping her chin in his hand, he kissed her. "I miss you whenever I'm away from you."

"You're sweet," she said. She kissed him back. "Now go — my toes are freezing."

He started to climb into the car but stopped and leaned over the car door as she walked away. "Hey, Bets, I have an idea."

She turned back, wrapping her arms even tighter around Megan. "It'd better be good."

"What would you think of my inviting Nephi and Jeanine over for dinner Saturday night?"

"That would be nice. Do you think they'll have any trouble finding a babysitter?"

"I mean the whole family. We could have our last cookout of the season."

"All those kids in my house?" Why did she have to

marry a man from a large family? Their opinions of what constituted too many children differed by about twelve.

"Oh, I'll set up some things to play with in the backyard. It'll be fun."

She didn't answer. She just looked unconvinced.

"Think about it." He climbed into the car. "Okay?"

That she could do, so she nodded her agreement, waved good-bye, and ran into the house, bouncing a laughing Megan.

If Paul had his way, they would probably have had six children by this time. He had grown up with six brothers and sisters and had loved it. Elizabeth envied him the happy childhood he had enjoyed, but she thought she could provide the same happiness for Megan with fewer numbers.

She swung Megan over the side of the playpen that was kept in the kitchen but grabbed her back up when she realized that Megan had clutched the baby ring and was sucking on it. "Oh, no-no, honey." She disentangled the chain from Megan's fist. "Okay. That's it," she said. "Let's go put Mommy's ring up before it gets lost or you get choked."

Upstairs, Elizabeth sat Megan on the floor and tossed her a brooch, a piece of costume jewelry, to play with. Then she sat down at her vanity. Before she laid the necklace into its satin compartment in her jewelry box, she held the ring up in front of her, wishing it could speak and tell her about the woman who had worn it before. She didn't really want to take it off, but she would rather it be safe until Megan was older. No chance anyone would show up claiming the ring — or her — anyway.

She rolled the tiny ring between her finger and her thumb, looking once more at the inside to where she could barely see the engraved initials — K. L. Were they her mother's? Maybe her grandmother's?

With a last sigh, she put the ring inside the compartment

and softly slid the drawer shut. She caught a glimpse of herself in the mirror and, thinking of what Paul would say if he saw her now, she lingered to stare at herself. She could almost hear Paul's words: "There are those sad eyes again. I thought we had gotten rid of those."

It was the sadness in her eyes that he said had attracted him to her at first. Back in his college days, Paul had loved challenges even more than now, so he had decided to take upon himself the task of ridding her eyes of that sadness. He had done a good job, too. The past few years, especially since Megan's birth, the sadness was hard to see, unless Elizabeth's thoughts were on her ring and the woman who had put it on her finger before giving her up.

Megan patted Elizabeth's leg, tearing Elizabeth away from her reflection in the mirror. "Hi, honey." She picked Megan up and buried her face in Megan's softness. Had her mother missed the moments and feelings that she now felt were so precious with Megan? Megan squirmed against her hold. "I guess I'll never know, will I, baby?"

She put Megan down and stood up to turn her back on the jewelry box. The ring would be safe there, and she had to get her thoughts together before her appointment this afternoon. Somehow she had to start thinking like a realtor again, even though the appointment was only for a lease-signing. A good place to start would be to find the name of the woman she was meeting. For some reason she remembered the Jesselene part, but where had she written her last name?

Picking Megan up, she shut the bedroom door behind her and, for the next few minutes at least, pushed the thoughts of the baby ring and the mother she would never know as far back in her mind as she could.

Elizabeth was enjoying her afternoon. It felt good to get out of her blue jeans and back into a suit that the editors of *Vogue* would certainly approve of. She had put her books and lists into the sporty blue BMW after she and Megan had come back from their morning walk. Organized and in control—that's how she liked to be every minute of her life. She had learned early in her childhood that the more she stayed in control, the less she could be hurt.

Megan settled down for a nap without complaining, and, as Gladys sank into an armchair in the den to watch her "story" on the soaps, Elizabeth left right on time. She was to meet Jesselene at the first of the available offices on her list.

When Elizabeth reached the office for lease, Jesselene was already there, which impressed Elizabeth. She hated waiting for tardy clients. Now she could possibly get back before Megan even realized she was gone.

"Hello. I'm Elizabeth Danforth," she said, proferring her hand. Jesselene clasped it in both of hers and was so grateful for Elizabeth's willingness to help that Elizabeth immediately wanted to. They stood outside for a few minutes, the noise of the traffic behind them and the warm afternoon sun on their shoulders, talking about what a beautiful fall they were having.

After a few minutes, Elizabeth said, "Well, are you ready to go in?"

"I sure am," Jesselene answered. "I have a good feeling about this afternoon. I think I'm going to find an office at last."

"I hope so." Elizabeth unlocked the door and ushered Jesselene inside.

Three offices and two hours later, Jesselene fell in love with an office. Elizabeth had to admit that her client had made a good choice.

"This is perfect," Jesselene said. "It's in an office building, so when the women come in for help, no one will know which office they're going to. They'll feel as if they have more privacy." She walked through what would be the waiting room, then down a tiny hall that had a smaller room on the left, a bathroom on the right, and a good-sized storage area at the end. "This is just the right size for the counseling office," she said, walking into the smaller room.

Elizabeth walked in, too, and sat down in one of the chairs, finding Jesselene's enthusiasm contagious. "I'm glad you like it," she said.

"It's perfect," Jesselene said again. "I'll have a telephone installed immediately, and it'll take only one good Saturday to move things in. Then we can open for business." She sat in a chair across from Elizabeth, absolutely glowing.

"What exactly will you be doing here?" Elizabeth asked.

"We're calling it TLC for Tender Loving Care," she answered. "We'll be helping any woman who feels that she needs help with a pregnancy or a new baby. We'll provide counseling and help arrange medical care. Then later after the baby is born, we'll help out with clothes and formula. Sort of a shoulder for a woman facing a problem pregnancy to lean on."

"What a wonderful thing to do, Mrs. Manning," Elizabeth said. "Having a baby is difficult enough without anyone to take care of you and give you support."

"Especially if you're young and unmarried," Jesselene said.

"Yes," Elizabeth said quietly. Her hand went to her throat and stroked it as if searching for something that wasn't there.

"Do you have children?" Jesselene asked.

"I have a baby girl. In fact," she said, smiling, "I happen to have quite a few pictures right here." She reached down into her leather shoulder bag to pull out a small album.

Jesselene took the album from her and opened it. "Oh, she's darling," she exclaimed. "You must adore her."

"We do," Elizabeth replied as Jesselene flipped through the pages.

"Babies are precious. That's why I have to get TLC going."

This must really be important to her, Elizabeth thought. She had wondered why a woman with a nice home and two teenage children would feel so compelled to help people she didn't even know. Elizabeth hoped to own her own successful real estate agency by the time Megan was in high school. She wanted enough people working for her so that she could be available whenever Megan needed her or whenever Paul called and wanted to jet off to some exotic place like Hawaii or Tahiti. She could throw a few things in a bag and leave, just like on those soap operas Gladys loved. Elizabeth suddenly noticed that Jesselene was talking to her, so she stopped daydreaming and started listening again. "Pardon me?" she said.

"I said that maybe you could volunteer a couple of nights

a month here," Jesselene said. "We'll need a lot of people if we're going to be open every night."

"Oh." Elizabeth smiled politely. "I don't know. I'll be awfully busy working part-time and taking care of Megan." She looked down to gather up her books, then glanced back up to see Jesselene looking at her with a kind but disappointed smile. Elizabeth immediately felt guilty. "But I'll be glad to help you get settled in this office, and I can handle any of the paperwork and leases."

"I appreciate it, dear." Jesselene stood up and patted Elizabeth on the hand. "You're real sweet."

"I'll call the owner and set a time when we can get together to sign the lease. I'll call you tonight, okay? Now I need to get home before the baby wakes up."

They walked through the waiting room again and out into the hall. As Elizabeth locked the door, she felt, for some reason she couldn't explain, as if she should do something nice for the woman still glowing beside her. "I'll look through Megan's clothes that she's outgrown and give you some of them to start out with. She had some real cute things."

"That would be wonderful," Jesselene said. Then she looked down at her watch. "I'd better go home too. My daughter is having a meeting at our home after school, and I promised I'd be there to hand out some snacks."

"That sounds good," Elizabeth said. She walked with Jesselene to the outer door of the building, then realized that she had left her shoulder bag inside the office. "I'll call you tonight," she promised Jesselene again and said goodbye.

She took only a moment to retrieve her shoulder bag. She paused in the office, picturing the waiting room full of teenage girls and older women hoping to be helped by that kind woman. Jesselene had said "my daughter" so lovingly too. My daughter, my daughter. No one had ever said that about her. For a few seconds, Elizabeth allowed herself to wonder where in the vast world was the one women who could honestly call her "my daughter." Then, as she had grown adept at doing, she pushed the thought back deep inside and walked out the door. But as she walked down the hall, she allowed herself to consider that maybe, if Paul didn't mind, she could volunteer at the TLC office one night a month. Maybe she could save one little girl the heartache of going through life never being called "my daughter" by anyone.

That evening, when Paul pulled into the driveway, Elizabeth was sitting on the side patio while Megan tossed blocks around in the playpen. Getting out of his car, he looked at his wife and felt his heart skip as it always did when he realized how much he loved her. He joined her, then bent down and kissed her. Megan was already standing, stretching her arms up for him and crying to be picked up, so he turned to his daughter and lifted her out of the playpen. He sat down with Megan across from Elizabeth.

"So, how was your first day back at work?" he asked.

She must have been waiting for his question because she immediately launched into a detailed description of her afternoon with Jesselene Manning.

"So, you were able to help her?" he asked as she slowed down.

"I think so. All we need to do is sign the lease," she said. "And it's for such a good cause."

"What is?" Paul asked, giving Megan a playful bounce on his knee.

"The reason she wants the office." She stood and picked up his briefcase. "She's starting an organization to help unwed mothers. And married women who need help with their pregnancies. Actually, anyone who needs help, I guess."

Paul didn't say anything, but he looked at her intently.

Elizabeth leaned over the playpen to grab a couple of toys and mumbled something Paul couldn't quite understand.

"What did you say, Bets?" he asked.

"Nothing much," she said. "Let's go in."

He was suddenly alert. "Tell me what you said."

"You'll just fuss."

"I will not. I'll fuss if you don't tell me."

"I said . . . " she started, then paused, " . . . maybe if there had been nice women like her around when I was a baby, Megan would have grandparents today."

"She has grandparents—my parents," he said carefully. He knew that wasn't what Bets really meant.

"I know."

He waited, but she didn't say more as she walked into the kitchen. Carrying Megan, he followed her through the door.

Elizabeth stopped at the kitchen counter, deep in thought. Finally, she said, as if thinking aloud, "I suppose what I really meant was that, if there had been nice people like this Jesselene back when my mother was in trouble, then maybe I wouldn't have grown up in foster homes, never knowing who my mother was."

Paul put Megan down on the floor and reached for Elizabeth. She moved away briefly, then suddenly turned back and slipped into Paul's arms. "Honey, I shouldn't have even said that. I have you and Megan and a beautiful new home. Your parents are wonderful. It's the first time in many years that I've been so happy."

Paul buried his face in her sweet-smelling hair. "I'm glad, sweetheart, because I'm happy too." He sighed, then held her back from him to look at her. "I know you'll always have an empty spot in your life because of your childhood. But now we have a family of our own, and we'll give Megan the kind of childhood you missed out on."

22

"You're sweet," she said, kissing him lightly on the cheek. "Now let's not talk about this anymore. You take care of Megan while I finish dinner."

As Paul watched her set the table, he remembered the time not too long ago when a conversation like the one they'd just had would have ended with her tears. She had become happier the last year—Megan had helped. Maybe now she would feel as if she had a place in the universe. In fact, maybe he should mention what Nephi had told him today—something about everyone being a child of God. It had sounded so comforting when they were talking about it. As he picked Megan up again and headed for the den, he decided against it. If given a choice between tending a baby, even one with dirty diapers, and discussing religion with Bets, he was no fool. He started upstairs for a diaper.

● ● ●

"It's just perfect," Jesselene said. She had already repeated that about six times since they'd climbed into the station wagon to drive to Country Gables for a celebration dinner. She had been describing the office since she had gotten home.

"That's real nice, Mom," Steve said.

"Can I work at the office sometimes, Mother?" Diane asked. She had asked several times before, but Jesselene had never given her a firm answer.

But this time she said, "I think that would be a great idea, Diane. You could help with the clothes and the baby furniture, and maybe this would help you see what a serious responsibility having a baby is."

"Mother," Diane said patiently, "I don't need a lecture. I want to help. I know a baby is a big responsibility."

"I know you do, dear. Anyway, I want you all to keep Saturday open to help at the office."

"Sure, Mom," Steve said. "I can help after my soccer game."

"I've got a stake meeting Saturday morning," Rowland said. "But I can fill the truck up after that. It'll be nice to finally get that furniture out of the garage."

Rowland hadn't said much since she had been home, but that was fine with Jesselene. Theirs was a very balanced marriage. She was the hare, always jumping around, getting involved first in one project, then in another, good at organizing and accomplishing. Rowland was the tortoise, steady and solid, planning and finishing all the detail work she had no time or patience for. In one busy week, after placing a big ad in the newspaper, she had filled the garage with baby cribs, cradles, and playpens, but Rowland was the one who had spent every evening in the garage fixing, painting, and repairing all of them. He kept her feet on the ground, and she kept him excited about life.

"Can we get dessert tonight, Mom?" Steve asked. Steve had a way of bringing Jesselene back to the important things in life.

"Sure," she said. "What's a celebration without dessert?"

"Not fattening," Diane mumbled.

When they pulled up in front of the restaurant, Jesselene finally ran out of breath. She reached for the door handle, but Rowland put his hand firmly on her shoulder.

"You go on in, kids, and get us a table," he said. "Your mother and I will join you in just a minute." As the children went ahead, he said, "Let's talk." Rowland looked quite serious.

Jesselene mentally reviewed her chattering of the last few minutes, but she couldn't remember any reason he should be so serious. She leaned back against her seat, letting go of the door handle. "Okay. About what?"

"About you and your TLC. I've never seen you so obsessed with a project."

"Oh, don't be silly," she said. "I've gone overboard on most of my projects." She hoped that would end the conversation, but his expression didn't change.

"I want to know," he said, "why all of a sudden you decided to even take on this particular crusade?"

"Don't you think helping unwed mothers is worthwhile?"

"You know I do," he said. "But you were so involved with the concert association and the hospital auxiliary, and then suddenly you gave that up."

"I just took some time off," she defended herself.

"But why now?"

Jesselene gazed at him. If she insisted, she knew that he would drop the subject—he never pushed her about anything. But she looked at him as intently as he was looking at her and realized that he didn't really expect her to answer. He already knew the answers. He wanted to know if she did, or, if she already knew, whether she was admitting them to herself.

"You're right," she said softly. "I'm doing it mostly for me."

"But, dear"—he said it so kindly that tears came to her eyes. "That was so long ago. You were so young."

Fifteen. She had been only fifteen. Long before she had joined the Church, long before she had known how painful consequences could be. "I know how young I was, Rowland. And I know I've been forgiven." Her baptism while she was in college had brought her the sweetness of forgiveness that she had yearned for.

"Then forgive yourself, Jess."

"I have, honey. I really have. But what if I can save some woman the same pain I suffered?"

"But I don't want working there to bring back all those feelings." He leaned over and took both her hands in his. "I don't want anything to hurt you."

"I know, and I appreciate it. But I can handle this. I *want* to do this—please give me your blessing."

He smiled. "You know I can't refuse you anything. But . . . " he said, pausing, " . . . I'll be watching you real close."

"You do that," she said. "I wouldn't want it any other way."

4

The midweek partners' meeting was nearing the end. Paul watched Ben face the assembled attorneys around the conference table and hold up both hands. "Anybody need anything else?" Ben asked.

Paul glanced down at his watch, hoping no one had anything to bring up. He had just enough time to talk to Nephi for a couple of minutes and then make it to his first appointment for the afternoon. Luckily, Paul thought, everyone shook their heads and began to stuff notes into their briefcases. Nephi was almost out of the room before Paul looked up. "Nephi," Paul called. "Wait up. I want to ask you something."

"Sure," he answered. "What can I do for you?"

Paul joined Nephi, and they walked from the conference room together. "I want to invite your family over for dinner Saturday night at our house," Paul said.

"The whole family?" Nephi asked. "Do you know how seldom our whole family gets invited to anyone's house?"

"I can imagine," Paul said, laughing. "But we want the package deal, all or none of you."

"Sounds good to me, but I'll have to ask Jeanine to make sure. I can call her from my office."

They arrived at Paul's office, and Paul reached in and placed his briefcase on a chair. He turned back to Nephi to find Nephi scrutinizing him. "You're sure Elizabeth knows how many children we have? Five?"

"Do you want to put me under oath? She knows. It's fine with her. I came from a family of seven kids myself."

"How about Elizabeth? Big family, too?"

Paul folded his arms across his chest and leaned back against the door before answering. "No, Bets wasn't quite so lucky with her family. She spent a lot of time in foster homes. But don't worry, she's looking forward to tomorrow night. So go call Jeanine, and let's get this on the calendar."

"Okay," Nephi said. "You've been sufficiently warned."

Paul watched his friend walk on down the hall, wondering why he had liked Nephi as soon as they had met. It almost seemed as if he'd known Nephi before — like *déjà vu*. Maybe he's similar to one of my brothers, Paul thought, though he couldn't put a finger on which one. With his slenderness and glasses, Nephi didn't look like any of the sturdy farming men Paul's three brothers had turned out to be.

He saw his client enquire at the secretary's desk, so he cut his musing short. Maybe by dinner on Saturday, he'd remember who Nephi reminded him of. Maybe then he'd also understand why he was even motivated to invite them all for dinner. He and Elizabeth had never had a couple with five children spend time at their home. It was certainly a first — one he hoped Bets would enjoy.

● ● ●

Saturday morning came with Elizabeth still in her bathrobe, curled up on the den couch beside Megan. They had both been up quite a bit of the night because of Megan's fever. Around two A.M., it had finally dipped below a hundred, and at last Megan and Elizabeth had fallen asleep.

Paul meanwhile was outside. He had already been in the backyard for at least two hours building a recreational park. He finished tying the volleyball net between two big trees, readjusted a couple of the croquet wickets that he had tripped over, and lined up a volleyball, a football, and two little baby balls on the patio before going back into the house to check on Megan and Elizabeth. He quietly shut the sliding doors when he saw that they were asleep and tiptoed over to put one finger on Megan's forehead to check the fever. She felt only slightly warm.

His fever check made Elizabeth open her eyes sleepily. "The doctor called back," she said. "I couldn't find you."

"I went to put air in our bicycle tires," he said. "What did he say?"

"He said to keep giving her the Tylenol and to call him back this evening if her fever goes real high. It might be a virus. If she doesn't get better soon, it could be something more serious, like an ear infection."

"Maybe I should call the Robertsons and postpone dinner," he said.

"After you've dragged every single thing in our basement that could possibly be fun into our backyard?" she said. "Forget it. I'm sure they've been around babies with a little fever before. She's probably just teething." She closed her eyes again, but then dragged them open and sighed. "I guess I need to get up and get some work done while she's sleeping."

"I'll do it. I promised that you wouldn't have to do anything. What do you need done?"

"Don't be silly. I don't mind them coming at all." The last couple of days, some of Paul's enthusiasm had rubbed off on her, and she was excited to see Jeanine again. She gently disentangled herself from Megan, who started sucking vigorously on her thumb again but didn't open her eyes. Sitting up on the couch, she shook her head to wake herself up. "I must look terrible."

Paul chuckled. "You look stunning." He tucked a pillow under Megan's head and pulled Elizabeth up from the couch.

She yawned, then said, "I think I'll go take a shower. Can you watch the baby?"

"Sure. I can see her from the kitchen."

"The kitchen?" Elizabeth asked suspiciously. "Why will you be in the kitchen?"

"I'm going to make one of my famous tossed salads to go with the steaks."

Elizabeth groaned. When Paul started chopping and dicing, there was no predicting what would wind up in the salad. "No anchovies this time," she said. "I hate anchovies."

"No anchovies," he promised.

About fifteen minutes later, when Elizabeth came back to the kitchen after showering and dressing, Paul was still immersed in salad-making. She poked around in the big salad bowl until he wiped his hands on the apron he was wearing and pulled her hands out of the bowl. "Don't peek."

Since she couldn't look, she sniffed. Sometimes his salads smelled deadlier than they actually looked.

"No blue cheese, either," he said. "I'm a man of my word."

"I trust you," she said, "except when it comes to salads." She walked over to the den door to make sure Megan was still asleep, then sat down on a stool at the bar and picked up a stray lettuce leaf to nibble on. "Did Megan wake up?"

"Didn't move," Paul said.

"Won't you miss mass tonight?" Elizabeth asked.

"I can go in the morning." He went on slicing tomatoes and added, as he always did, "Maybe you can go too."

"Maybe," she said, as she always did. She admired his faithfulness in going to mass every weekend, especially without her support. She knew he would love to have her and Megan go with him. Maybe she would one of these days. She had thought about it through the years — she just hadn't done it yet. "Depends on how Megan feels." He would know that wasn't the truth, but he was too good to say anything about it.

She had prayed when she was little. Every single night for years she had knelt beside her bed and asked God with all the fervency she could to bring her mommy back to her and take her to live in a real home with a real family. But it had never happened. Then she had become a teenager and, like many other teenagers, began to question everything and believe nothing. She had stopped praying, and, somewhere so deep in her heart that she didn't even have to think about it very often, she had promised God that, when he gave her back her mother, she would believe in him again.

That hadn't happened through the years, and her lack of faith and of dependence upon any higher being had long ago become a way of life. Only to Paul had she been able to relinquish any part of her independence and self-reliance. She had even fought that for months until she had to admit she was crazy in love with the good-looking second-year law student. But even that love had its limits, and going to church with him was one of them.

As she checked to see if the steaks were thawing on schedule, a terrible thought suddenly occurred to her. "Oh no, Paul, is it the Mormons who don't eat beef?"

"No, silly, that's another church. And it's pork."

She was impressed. She didn't know he knew so much about the Mormons.

"Besides no alcohol or tobacco, the only thing they don't do is drink coffee or tea."

"No coffee?" The thought was so staggering to Elizabeth that she grabbed the edge of the counter for support.

"Or tea."

"I'd die."

"You might."

"So how do you know all this, honey?" she asked.

"You know how intelligent I am," he joked.

"The truth, counselor."

"Actually," he said, "I asked. I thought they didn't eat meat either. In fact, that's why I went and bought all this salad stuff."

She reached into the cookie jar and pulled out a cellophane package. "How about if my Twinkie and I go check on the baby?" She grabbed up the lease contract she needed to look over for Mrs. Manning and went into the den. Megan was still sleeping, but when Elizabeth gently felt her little forehead, it seemed just a little warmer than it had been before. Maybe she should call the doctor again and meet him at the hospital. No, stop worrying, she told herself. Just because I'm a first-time mother, I don't have to act like one. Besides what better company could we be having than the parents of five children? Elizabeth smiled to herself. Jeanine would know exactly what was wrong with Megan. And maybe, if they survived the eating of Paul's salad, she could ask her.

● ● ●

Elizabeth had just laid Megan down in her crib when she saw out the window that the Robertsons had pulled up in their van. Megan's temperature was up a little but not enough to warrant a call to the doctor. Since Megan had slept most of the morning and skipped her afternoon nap, Elizabeth had given her baby daughter another dose of Tylenol, hoping she would take a short nap and sleep through most of the dinner ahead.

Patting Megan with one hand, she peeked through the curtain as Paul walked down the front sidewalk to greet them. She was anxious to get to know them better since Paul seemed to like Nephi so much. Paul had tried to explain why he wanted to invite them over but had finally admitted that he really didn't know.

Megan soon fell asleep. Elizabeth flipped on the intercom and quietly closed the door. After looking in the mirror and passing her inspection, she headed for the patio, where she heard all the voices. "Hi," she said when she got there. "I was up putting the baby to bed. She's not feeling very well."

"That's what Paul was telling us," Jeanine said. "I hope it's not too serious."

"She's probably just teething," Elizabeth said. "In fact, I told Paul I might have you look at her. You must know everything about kids." She looked down at the line of kids between Nephi and Jeanine. They were standing quietly, to Elizabeth's amazement.

Paul followed her eyes. "Are they always so quiet?"

Nephi and Jeanine laughed. "No," they said together.

"Hi," Paul said to the children. He started down the line shaking hands.

"This is Emily and Jared and Brett and Julianne," Nephi said. "And Sarah," holding up the baby girl on his arm.

"Isn't she cute?" Elizabeth said. "Megan will like playing with her when she wakes up."

"Well." Paul clapped his hands together, then pointed to the backyard. "Would you kids like to play? I got a bunch of things out I think you might like."

"Yes," they said unanimously and went running.

Paul turned to Nephi. "How about it, Nephi? We could

33

play a game of croquet with the kids while the coals are heating."

"Sounds good." He handed Sarah to Jeanine. "Maybe you can fill me in on some of these judges while I beat you."

"I can help you out with the judges even while you're losing."

They both laughed and, bending down to pick up two croquet balls, left Jeanine and Elizabeth on the patio.

"Your home is beautiful," Jeanine said.

"Thank you," Elizabeth said. "We fell in love with it the first time we saw it."

"It must be fun being a realtor and seeing so many homes every day."

"It really is," Elizabeth said.

They sat for a few minutes and watched the croquet game in the yard. Paul and Nephi looked as if they were spending more time dodging the children's balls than actually playing.

"Is there anything I can help you with?" Jeanine asked.

"Sure." Elizabeth got up, listening a minute to the intercom beside the patio door. "I'm going to go check on Megan, and then we can set the tables."

"Can I put Sarah in the playpen?" Jeanine asked.

"Of course, that's why it's there. But there may not be room for her. Paul pretty well filled it up with toys."

Jeanine cleared a space in the middle and put a delighted Sarah down. "Show me the dishes and I'll start."

"Right in here." Elizabeth led Jeanine into the kitchen, showed her where the dishes were already set out on the counter, then went upstairs. When she peeked through the door, Megan was awake but lay very still. Elizabeth stood there for a minute, but Megan didn't cry, so Elizabeth assumed that she had woken up when the door opened. After checking to see that the intercom was still on, Elizabeth shut the door and went downstairs, sure that Megan would go back to sleep.

By the time Elizabeth reached the patio, Jeanine was well on her way to having the outdoor table set. The men had started putting the steaks on the grill, comparing successful grilling techniques. From then on, conversation stayed light, interspersed with laughter as the Robertsons entertained them with stories of situations their children had gotten into, some of which made Elizabeth just a little bit apprehensive about ever letting Megan out of her playpen again.

"So, tell me," Paul said as they finished eating. "Didn't you tell me that you used to live out this way for a couple of years?"

"Yes," Nephi answered. "I spent two years in this area serving a mission for our church. I actually never lived in Waynesboro—just visited—but I did spend about four months in Charlottesville."

"So that's how you know about UVA," Elizabeth said to Jeanine. She hoped the conversation would switch to Jeanine returning to school.

"Yes," Jeanine said. "Nephi just loved it out here. He always wanted to come back, and when the job showed up in the paper, he got all excited."

"So here we are," Nephi said.

"Tell me about a mission," Paul said. "Were you one of those guys in suits who ride bicycles and knock on doors?"

Elizabeth did not want to talk about church, especially if Nephi had been trained as a professional missionary. She'd never forget the night one of the nuns had cornered her at a Brunswick stew social at Paul's church. She started stacking dishes to look too busy to join in.

"I sure was," Nephi answered.

"So what exactly did you do?" Paul asked.

Enough already, Elizabeth thought.

Nephi put his fork down and folded his arms on the table. It looked to Elizabeth like serious conversation was about to start.

"Well," he said, "we went into people's homes and taught them the gospel of Jesus Christ. And that the true church of Jesus Christ has been restored to the earth through the prophet Joseph Smith."

"Wow," Paul said, laughing a little. "That sounds pretty heavy. I've always thought that my church had the corner on belief in the true church."

"Are you Catholic?" Nephi asked.

"Yes," Paul answered.

"He attends mass every week," Elizabeth offered.

"So who is this Joseph Smith?" Paul asked. "I thought Brigham Young started your church."

"A lot of people do," Nephi explained. "But Joseph Smith was chosen as a boy to restore the Lord's church on the earth again."

Where had it been? Elizabeth wondered, but she didn't ask because she was smart enough to know that she couldn't hold her own in a conversation on religion. Then she heard a faint cry on the intercom. Even though it had to be from Megan, it didn't sound like her waking-up cry.

"Excuse me," Elizabeth said. "Megan must be awake." She smiled nicely at Jeanine again — she really did like her — and walked inside, listening as she did to some fantastic-sounding story about gold plates under a rock. She wondered as she walked up the stairs how she could change the subject when she went down again.

But once she saw Megan all other thoughts fled from her mind. She ran across the room, calling Paul through the intercom as she went. Megan was lying exactly as Elizabeth had left her nearly two hours before, eyes wide open and little cheeks bright red with fever.

Elizabeth grabbed her up. "Megan, baby, you're burning up. Paul, Paul," she called again.

She held her close as she tried to remember where she had put the thermometer. Before she could find it, Paul ran into the room, followed close behind by Jeanine and Nephi.

"What's wrong, sweetheart? Is Megan okay?" Paul asked anxiously.

"She's burning up, Paul. She's never been so hot." She held Megan out to Paul, who took her and cradled her in his arms. She lay back glassy-eyed without protest.

"Here, let me feel," Jeanine said, putting her hand on Megan's forehead.

"Have any of your children ever had such a high fever?" Elizabeth asked. She finally found the thermometer.

"Brett's is always high when he's sick," Jeanine said reassuringly. "Once it was a hundred and five and a half."

"Do you think Megan's is that high? What should I do?" A fear she had never known was tightening around her heart and choking her.

"Well, let's take her temperature, and then we'll sponge her off if it's real high."

Elizabeth let Jeanine take Megan and lay her down on the dressing table. "Here," Jeanine said. "I'll undress her."

"Okay," Elizabeth said. Jeanine acted so calm and competent that Elizabeth relaxed a little.

"I'll go watch our kids," Nephi said. "That grill is still hot." He slapped Paul on the back. "Call me if you need me."

"Thanks," Paul said.

"Paul," Jeanine said. "Go run some water in the tub. Not warm but not too cool."

Elizabeth stroked Megan as she stared at the mercury in the thermometer. Jeanine pulled it out and squinted down at it. "It's a hundred and four and a half," she announced.

"Oh no," Elizabeth said. "It's never been that high."

"Take her and put her in the tub and sponge her off," Jeanine said calmly. "And let's give her some Tylenol. Then we'll decide what to do next."

Talking calmly, Jeanine stayed beside Elizabeth, but Elizabeth's hands shook as she bathed the baby. Megan didn't protest as she was sponged with the lukewarm water. After a while, her cheeks were no longer cherry red, and she felt cooler to the touch. When they wrapped her in a towel and took her temperature again, it had gone down two-and-a-half degrees.

"Oh, thank you so much," Elizabeth said. "I never would have known what to do."

"Oh, yes you would have," Jeanine said. "But I think you'd better see the doctor before it goes up again."

"He's already expecting us," Paul said, joining them again. "I called while you were washing Megan." He was as colorless as Elizabeth felt.

After diapering Megan, Elizabeth followed Paul and Jeanine down to the kitchen where Nephi and the children were busily cleaning up. "You didn't have to clean up," she said. "We must have ruined your evening. I'm sorry."

"We've had a great time," Nephi said. "Is the baby okay?"

"Much better," Elizabeth said. "Thanks to your wife. But we're taking her to the hospital."

"Will she have to get a shot?" Jared asked.

"I hope not," Elizabeth said. "But thanks for asking. That's real sweet."

"We prayed for her while you were gone," little Julianne said. "So I know she'll get well."

Nephi patted her on the head and pulled her over to him. "She'll get well real fast."

"You said a prayer for her?" Paul asked. He didn't dare look at Elizabeth, but that touched him.

There was a short silence—only slightly embarrassed.

Then Nephi looked over at Jeanine. "Well, dear," he said. "We need to be going so they can take care of the baby."

"Yes." Jeanine turned to Elizabeth. "Thank you so much for having us over. We really enjoyed it. When we get everything unpacked at our house, you'll have to come to see us."

"We'd love to," Elizabeth replied. "But I feel like we need to have you over again when we don't have to go rushing off to the hospital."

"You're talking to parents of five children," Jeanine said. "We know all about rushing off to hospitals."

"I still don't believe you have five kids," Elizabeth said, shaking her head.

"Look at the cupcake plate," Nephi said. "It's empty."

They laughed again, then Nephi and Jeanine started pushing kids out the door. Paul and Elizabeth walked with them to the van.

"Thank you so much for your help," Elizabeth said again. "I'm so glad you all were here tonight."

"I'm glad I could help," Jeanine said. "I'll call later and see how Megan is."

As the Robertsons pulled out of the driveway, Paul opened their car door for Elizabeth. "Aren't they wonderful people?" he asked.

"They really are, honey. I'm so glad they were here when Megan got so sick."

"Me, too."

Paul was quiet for a few minutes as he drove. Then he asked, "Did Nephi remind you of one of my brothers?"

She thought, trying to make a connection between one of Paul's big, dark, and often loud brothers and the quieter, blond Nephi, but she couldn't make out any similarities. "No," she finally said, "not a single one."

"Me neither," Paul said. "But I've known someone like him sometime in my life. Funny, isn't it?"

Elizabeth nodded, but her thoughts were on Jeanine. She wondered if she would ever be the confident mother that Jeanine was. Eight months ago, she hadn't even known the little girl beside her, and now she was so scared that something could be wrong with her. Perhaps Megan was the reason that Paul had felt so strongly about having the Robertsons over for supper tonight. They were sent over to help her baby. But that's ridiculous, she reprimanded herself. Sent by whom?

5

Jesselene slid into the back row of chairs in the Relief Society room before the prelude music even began. After so many years of sitting on back rows with her noisy children, she still automatically headed for those rows. There she could always find babies to drool on her finger or pull at her necklace. But no babies were there yet, so she sat back and let the first notes of the music wash over her in quiet waves.

The room began to fill up with sisters and diaper bags. She knew most of them so well that coming to church was almost like attending a family reunion. Speaking first to one, then to another in hushed voices, she was a little surprised but delighted when a newcomer to the ward whom she had spoken to only once or twice slipped in beside her, baby on one arm, diaper bag on the other.

"Sister Manning?" she asked.

"Hello, dear," Jesselene said. "Jeanine Robertson, right?"

"I didn't know if you'd remember me." She took a minute to situate baby and bag before she turned back to Jesselene. "I think what you're doing is wonderful, Sister

Manning, and I'd like to volunteer a couple of nights a month."

"We'd love to have you," Jesselene replied. "We can work around your schedule any way that's best for you." The baby caught sight of Jesselene's gold bracelet, so she held out her arm for the baby to play with it.

"I have five little ones, so evening hours when my husband is home would probably be best."

The Relief Society president stepped up to the podium as Jesselene pulled some handouts from her purse to hand to Jeanine. "Thank you so much," she whispered. "With all those little children, you'd be hard pressed to find open time. It would have been much easier to ignore my plea for help."

"Well," Jeanine said, smiling, "easier isn't always best."

What a nice sister, Jesselene thought, opening the hymnbook and offering it to Jeanine. She would tell her about the training sessions at the end of the meeting. The Relief Society president had told Jesselene that she could have a few minutes to speak. But for now, as the strains of "Because I Have Been Given Much" filled the room, she thought about how her dream was becoming real. The happiness in her heart mixed with the music, and she felt as if it were surrounding every sister and filling every corner of the room.

After the meetings, as Diane and Steve piled into the car, Jesselene smiled across at Rowland. "So seven sisters signed up to volunteer, and several more said they'd call me later this week." She got in and locked the car door, then turned to Steve and Diane in the back. "Seatbelts on?"

"Yes, Mother," Diane said.

"Sure," Steve said. "I'm starving."

"Sister Carlisle said that she would teach the Young

Adults how to crochet baby afghans, and we could donate them to TLC," Diane said.

"Yeah, Mom," Steve said. "I bet some of the guys would help fix the cribs and junk. And I could borrow Dad's truck and pick up things. J.C. would help."

"You and J.C. and my new truck?" Rowland laughed. "I say let's keep our heads about us and not do anything we'll regret later. Diane crocheting and you borrowing my truck sort of stretches the imagination. Right, Jess?"

"Sure," she said absentmindedly, peering out her window. "Now if I could just get that nice Elizabeth Danforth to work some." Suddenly she turned to grab Rowland's arm. "Turn there, Rowland. Quick." She pointed to a street almost beside them on the right.

"What's wrong?" Steve asked.

"Mother!" Diane exclaimed, grabbing onto the back of the seat for balance as Rowland turned sharply.

"I want to show you where that wonderful realtor Elizabeth lives." She rummaged through her purse for the card Elizabeth had given her. By the time she found it, they were just a few houses away from the address. "There — on the left."

"That's beautiful," Diane said.

"You know someone who lives in that kind of house, Mom?" Steve asked. "I'm impressed."

"Would you like to pull up and look in the windows?" Rowland asked.

"Sure," Steve said.

"Of course not," Jesselene said. "Just drive by — slowly. She's the nicest person."

Straining their necks to watch as long as they could, they followed the curve of the road, and the house disappeared from their sight.

"Don't you think she would work a couple of nights a month, hon'?" Jesselene asked Rowland.

He smiled over at her. "Of course, dear. I'm sure she would."

"I thought so."

"Mom, could we get home?" Steve asked. He clutched his stomach. "I'm starving."

"Sure, hon'." Jesselene scribbled down Elizabeth's name onto the list, then added two stars beside it. That would be her project for the week. First she would get Elizabeth to sign up to volunteer. Then she would convert her. Then her family. And then the whole neighborhood. She laughed inwardly at herself, knowing that she was doing just what she had promised Rowland she wouldn't do — get all carried away. Come back to earth, Jess. Back to Sunday and starving sons.

● ● ●

"That was an interesting conversation," Paul said. He put down the last piece of the Sunday paper he had just finished reading in bed. Bets had been reading it, too, until she had gotten a phone call. "First it was about refrigerator cords, then you were trying to convince whoever it was that you couldn't do something. Then it sounded as if they convinced you that you could, and somehow I'm going to help you decide whether you can or not." He had tried for the last twenty minutes to piece together her phone call, but it was beyond him.

"Pretty close," Elizabeth said.

"Was it that client of yours?" he asked.

"Jesselene Manning," Elizabeth answered. "Yes. The refrigerator won't fit where there's a plug, so I have to ask the owner if it's okay to have some rewiring done. It shouldn't be a problem."

"What can't you do, then?"

"Volunteer at the office."

"The unwed mothers' office?"

"TLC," she said. She punched her pillow around a couple of times before looking up at Paul very nonchalantly. "She wants me to volunteer two nights a month there."

"Is that so? Doing what, exactly?"

"Giving out baby clothes and formula and just generally helping women who need help with having babies."

It didn't sound like anything Bets had ever been interested in before, so he turned the football game up and directed his attention to that. "You're not qualified for that type of thing anyway."

"Well," she said in a funny tone of voice, "there's a training class you have to take. Thursday and Friday night."

Paul realized that the funny tone was possible interest and turned to his wife with a questioning look on his face. "You're not considering it, are you?"

"I don't know."

He turned the volume down. "You've never been interested in volunteer things before."

"I buy Girl Scout cookies," she said defensively.

"Oh, yeah," he said. He waited through another Cowboys' touchdown before he turned back to her. She was hugging her pillow and staring into space. Unable to resist her unusual pensiveness, he reached over to stroke her hair. "So why would you want to do this?"

"Like I told you once," she said—too casually, he thought—"maybe if someone had helped whoever my mother is—or was—then maybe I'd have a mother today."

"Bets." He picked up her hand and played with her wedding band. "Maybe you should just get used to working again and then see what happens."

"So you're saying I can't?"

"Wait a minute," he said, laughing. "I know better than to tell you not to do something."

"Well, I probably won't anyway."

The game got a little more exciting, so he dropped the subject until there was a lag in the action. Finally he asked, "Well, have you decided about working at that place, sweetheart?"

"TLC, Paul. And why are you so interested?"

"I'm always interested in what you do, Bets." She was sure testy, he thought. He waited for an answer to his question, but it didn't look as if she would answer. "What are you going to do, then?"

"About what?"

He would try to be patient. "About working at TLC."

"I haven't decided."

He watched as she reached over to snap off the light, then put his hand on her shoulder. "Bets, can I ask you something?"

"Yes, dear." But she didn't turn around.

"What if a young girl, really young, were to come to you and ask you to help her find a home for her baby? Could you do that?"

Silence. Then—"If she could find a wonderful family who would love the baby and give it all the things she couldn't. I could do that." Silence again. "Besides, things are different now. There are thousands of couples wanting to adopt babies. Babies don't go into foster homes."

"But what if the mother promises not to reveal her identity to the child? Many adopted children don't find out who their natural parents are."

"Well, I haven't even decided if I want to help Jesselene. I have to think about Megan too."

Paul hesitated only a moment before saying, "If you want to work a couple of nights a month, I would make sure I was home to take care of her."

That got her to turn around and smile. "That's real sweet, Paul." She reached for his hand, then snuggled down into her pillow.

He watched her go to sleep almost instantly — motherhood had given her that ability — but he lay awake, wondering if he had done her a favor by volunteering to babysit. Maybe that kind of work would help scare out some of those ghosts that were still within her. Or it could call some back. But who could tell? Just when he thought he had her all figured out, she did something that threw him off-balance again. He tried to turn his attention back to the game, but he found it difficult to concentrate.

CHAPTER

6

Even an hour's wait in the doctor's office Tuesday morning didn't spoil Elizabeth's good mood. She did worry a little, though, as the doctor looked first in Megan's right ear, then in the left, pursed his lips together and hm-m-m'd, and looked back in the first ear. "Anything wrong?" she asked him.

"Nope," he answered. "Looks good. Of course, be sure to give her all the rest of the antibiotic."

"I will," she promised. She was determined not to let Megan have a relapse. She was going to be as cool, calm, and collected as Jeanine. Without that mob of children, of course.

After the examination and out in the BMW, she buckled Megan in, then took a moment to enjoy the autumn beauty of the mountains surrounding Waynesboro. People from all over the country came to the Blue Ridge Parkway each fall to see the beauty of the foliage. "Aren't the leaves pretty?" she asked Megan.

Odd how things worked out. If anyone had told Elizabeth three or four years ago that she would be enjoying conversation with an eight-month-old, she wouldn't have believed them. But at this moment she was happy to be right where she was.

Her route took her past the office she had rented to Jesselene. She thought that she recognized Jesselene's station wagon out front. Impetuously she pulled into a parking place next to the wagon. "Let's go visit a minute, Megan," she said. She unbuckled the baby, then hoisted her out of the car. Turning around, she came face-to-face with Jesselene, who had just emerged from the office building.

"Well, hello, hon'," Jesselene said to Elizabeth. She patted Megan on the back. "Oh, she is adorable, Elizabeth. Prettier even than her pictures." Concern crossed her face. "There isn't a problem with the office, is there?"

"No, of course not," Elizabeth assured her. "Megan and I were just out doing some errands, and we happened to drive by."

"Good. I was worried for a minute there." She put a hand over her heart and sighed. "I thought that maybe the owners had decided not to rent to us after all—or they had changed their minds about the rewiring."

"Nope, we just came to visit."

Jesselene held the door open for them. "Then come on in and see what I've done to the place."

When Elizabeth walked into the office, she could hardly believe that it was the same place. With a comfortable couch, two Boston rockers with afghans folded neatly on the backs, and a coffee table on which was placed a mixture of current women's magazines, it looked like someone's living room.

Before Elizabeth could say anything, Jesselene reached down to plump the pillows on the couch. "I was just bringing in the plants, so it doesn't look quite like it's going to when I finish."

"I think it's beautiful," Elizabeth said sincerely. "Where

did you get all this furniture so quickly? And get it moved in?"

"Oh, a few friends of mine rummaged through their attics and basements Saturday. And one friend of mine who is elderly crochets afghans for church bazaars. She begged me to let her donate these. A sweet, sweet person. You'll have to meet her sometime." She moved a few philodendrons around on the end tables. "Then another friend of mine has a small greenhouse, and she brought me a couple of plants yesterday. And, to answer your second question, my husband and son helped me move the furniture in Saturday night."

"Well, it really looks nice," Elizabeth said again.

"I haven't had a chance to do too much with the office area." Jesselene started down the hall. "Come on back, though."

The office held a big comfortable rocking chair and a long table stacked with framed cross-stitch and needlepoint pictures. Elizabeth picked them up and looked at them one by one. "Where did you get all these beautiful pictures?" She touched one that was an especially lovely cross-stitching of a mother rocking a baby, with the words "I am a child of God" beneath it. Someone had put a lot of love and work into the pictures.

"Oh, I did them back a couple of years ago when I had surgery and had to do a lot of recuperating. I'm planning to put them in a nursery for my grandchildren one of these days." She reached into the desk and pulled out a framed photograph. "Here's my family."

"What a nice-looking family," Elizabeth said.

Jesselene took the picture from Elizabeth and looked down at it. "You remind me of my daughter, Diane. You both have such pretty soft brown hair." She put the picture back in the drawer. "So sit down and try out the rocking chair."

"It's so comfortable," she said, rocking Megan. She glanced down at her watch, amazed at how late it had gotten to be. It was almost time for Megan's medicine, and she supposed that she should be getting home to put Megan down for a nap. She stroked Megan's hair, which smelled like baby shampoo, then looked up to see Jesselene looking intently at her.

"Have you decided yet about signing up for volunteer work two or three times a month?" Jesselene asked. "You could come to one of our training sessions this week."

That's a good question, Elizabeth thought. Now if I could just think of a good answer. The one she came up with surprised even herself. "Will you be trying to get the girls to put their babies up for adoption?"

Jesselene looked puzzled for a moment, then answered after some thought, "I'll be the first to admit that's a difficult situation. But it will depend a lot on the individual's circumstances. Our role will be to help the girls make the decisions that're best for them and then to help them follow through. If they do decide on adoption, we'll work closely with the adoption agencies to make sure the babies go to good, loving homes." She shook her head and looked a little sad. "There are so many people wanting babies and unable to have them."

Elizabeth was about to make some excuse why she couldn't come, but suddenly she felt that she couldn't stand to have Jesselene disappointed in her. "What nights are the classes?"

"You'd consider it, then?" Jesselene said happily.

"To tell you the truth," she said, "I had already talked about it to Paul."

"That's wonderful. The classes are Thursday and Friday nights for probably two weeks. A director of a similar organization over in Charlottesville will be teaching, plus a counselor from Social Services. Here." She handed Elizabeth a flier with the information on it, which Megan immediately grabbed and began sucking. "Are you hungry, sweetie?" Jesselene laughed, handing Elizabeth another one.

"It is her lunchtime." Elizabeth looked over the flier carefully.

"Do you really think you can come?" Jesselene asked. "I'd love to have your help." Then she laughed again. "I'm sorry. My husband says I'm too pushy sometimes. I think he's right."

"That's okay. I'll take this home and think about it. I'm usually not the volunteering type, but for some reason this appeals to me." You know why it does, she thought. Be honest. At least to yourself.

"Well, that's all I can ask," Jesselene said. "Just give me a call if you have any questions."

Elizabeth stood up to leave, shifting Megan to her shoulder. "I will." Then on impulse, "Maybe I could work with you a few nights until I was sure what I was doing." Jesselene seemed like the kind of person who could handle any situation that arose.

"That would be fine, hon'," she answered.

Jesselene walked with them out to the car, watched as Elizabeth buckled Megan into her car seat, then walked around to the driver's side with Elizabeth. Elizabeth reached for the handle, but to her surprise, Jesselene reached out and caught her in a hug. "Thank you so much for stopping by, dear," Jesselene said.

"My pleasure," Elizabeth said. It *was* my pleasure, she thought as she drove away. If Jesselene ran her home anything like she had organized that office, coming home from school and from work every evening must be nice. She laughed to herself. Maybe she'd agree to volunteer at TLC if Jesselene would promise to invite her over for dinner one night. But then, maybe her one fault was that she was a terrible cook.

• • •

Paul hung up his office phone after talking to Bets, relieved that the doctor had declared Megan restored to health but a little uneasy about the conversation following the one about Megan. It had started out simply enough. "Nephi asked me if we'd like to come over Saturday night and have some Mexican food. Jeanine's a real Mexican gourmet cook." Then there'd been no answer from Bets's end of the line. "Does that suit you?" he had asked.

"I guess so," she'd answered.

"Great!" he said. He loved enchiladas. "About six?"

"Why so soon?" she asked then.

"Seven then?" If she didn't want to, he thought, why didn't she just say so?

"No, I mean," she had said, "so soon after we had them over."

"I don't know. I guess we're the only people they know so far. And I like them."

"Okay, let's go, then," she said.

"You're sure?"

"Yes," she had said.

Paul played with a pen for a while, thinking about his conversation with Bets. He wondered if he should have told her that Nephi planned to also show them a video about the Mormon church. It hadn't seemed like a good time to tell her. Why was Bets still so uptight about any religion?

He didn't even know why he was interested in these Mormons. Maybe interested wasn't the best word. Fascinated? Not that either. Drawn to? No. But he definitely was interested. Of course, he'd always been a Catholic, but it wouldn't hurt to check out what the Mormons believed. And the Robertsons really seemed to believe many startling things: angels in the nineteenth century, buried golden books, teenage prophets.

He should have told her about the video. Mulling the consequences of withholding evidence and suppressing testimony from a wife, he decided upon an alternative to actually facing her with the information. Instead of warning her about them and their video, he'd warn them about her.

A moment later, he poked his head into Nephi's office. "Very busy?"

"Oh, come on in, Paul," Nephi said. "Just doing some research." He marked the place in the book in front of him before closing it, then sat back in his chair. "What can I do for you?"

Paul leaned against the door frame, his arms folded. "Nothing really. I just talked to Bets, and she said Saturday night would be fine with her."

"Great."

"But I just thought I'd warn you. Bets might not be too interested in that video about the Mormon church." He searched for words that wouldn't offend. "She's never really been interested in any religion."

"Isn't she Catholic too?"

He laughed. "No, unfortunately."

"She doesn't mind you being a faithful Catholic?"

"No. She knew what I was when she married me, and we had an understanding when we got married. It's worked out well so far, though I keep hoping she'll become interested." He laughed again. "Of course, my mother has never forgiven me for not marrying a good Catholic girl like all my other brothers did."

Nephi seemed curious. "Does she lean toward any church?"

"Actually, she leans as far away as possible from any church."

"Why?"

Paul had never tried to explain his wife's beliefs to anyone before, but then no one had ever been interested. He decided to give it a try. "Her feelings toward religion have something to do with her childhood. She grew up in a lot of different foster homes, and I think she's been trying to punish God since that time for not giving her a mother and father." That sounded so harsh. "Maybe not punish . . . but I think she still has a lot of hurt left over and won't forgive God for her childhood."

"Hmm" was all Nephi said.

"So I don't know how she'll react to a video about your church."

"I'm glad you told me," Nephi finally said. "As I told you—we believe that we are all children of our Heavenly Father. Maybe if she could understand that, she would feel as if she belonged to a family of her own and could feel God's love."

That sounded good, Paul thought. Like something a priest or a minister would say. "Maybe so," he agreed. "Yeah, that makes sense."

"Why don't we play it by ear Saturday night? If Elizabeth doesn't want to see a video, then we won't worry about it."

That seemed reasonable. "Sounds good," he said.

"We've also got some excellent tapes about families. Maybe she'll be more interested in one of those. Okay?"

"All right." It did sound easy. He really hoped that Bets would agree to see one of the tapes.

The plan continued to sound just fine all the way back to his office until he sat down. What he had just agreed to suggest to Bets washed over him, and he groaned. Looking over at the picture of Bets and Megan on his desk, he practiced explaining it to her. "Look, sweetheart, it sounded good when he suggested it to me, and if you don't want to see it, just say so. Okay?" She looked agreeable enough in the picture, standing before a Christmas tree and rocking

55

horse. So he grabbed a folder and went back to work before she changed her expression.

As he worked, Paul kept remembering snatches of what Nephi had told him the past few weeks. Nephi's words always seemed to make sense, striking a familiar chord within him, almost as if he knew what Nephi knew, as if he were remembering things that had somehow been just beyond the grasp of his memory.

One thing he was sure of, though. If ever there was a day that called for coming home with flowers for Bets, it was today.

7

Elizabeth walked nervously down the hallway. Despite the butterflies in her stomach, Elizabeth felt a warm invitation coming from the sound of women's voices and the odor of something tangy emanating from the TLC office. Two women had come through the outside door behind her, so she couldn't hesitate too long. She pulled off her white gloves, smoothed her hair, and walked into a roomful of women she did not know.

About twenty women were sitting and standing throughout the room, most of them holding doughnuts and cups of steaming punch that smelled like cinnamon and apples. Jesselene stood behind a card table covered entirely with pamphlets and handouts, talking to a nicely dressed woman, who Elizabeth guessed must be the speaker. When Jesselene saw Elizabeth, though, she waved and came right over to her.

"Hi, Elizabeth," she said. "I'm so glad you could come. How is that sweet baby?"

"She's glad to be with her daddy tonight." Her voice dropped to a whisper. "I don't know anyone here." Could

Jesselene tell? Was the old insecurity of being the only one who didn't belong obvious?

"Well then, I'll introduce you." Before Elizabeth even had time to consider backing out through the door, Jesselene had pulled her over to an older woman sitting in the rocking chair. "Myrtle, this is Elizabeth," Jesselene said. "Can you keep an eye on her and introduce her around? She's the wonderful realtor who got this office for us. And, Elizabeth, Myrtle is the woman who crocheted all these afghans."

"They're beautiful," Elizabeth said sincerely.

With a pat and a smile, Jesselene went back to her table, leaving Elizabeth feeling warmer and more welcome. In the next few minutes, she met several of the people there. Then she sat down for the start of the program.

She had decided before coming tonight that she would be impartial and aloof from whatever might take place. Before she actually committed herself to anything official, she was going to very rationally and unemotionally check things out. But by the time Jesselene had spoken for only a few minutes, Elizabeth was trying to swallow a lump in her throat.

She glanced around, finding that several other women in the room were wiping their eyes. Jesselene, her voice thick with emotion, related several stories of girls who had desperately needed the help of an organization such as TLC. She ended with the words "Perhaps a caring voice, some loving support, a helping hand would have made the difference in their lives."

Elizabeth was so deep in thought, considering the possibility that her mother might not have wanted to give her up but had been forced to, that most of what the next speaker said washed right over her without registering. But the mention of adoption brought her back to the present. She focused on the discussion of the process of adoption.

Listening to the woman's concern for the well-being of both mother and baby, Elizabeth knew that she could go home and tell Paul that yes, she could support a young girl in her decision to give up her baby. She found herself wishing that a woman so kind had been responsible for finding her a home.

Two speakers later, as the meeting ended with a question-and-answer period, Elizabeth sat quietly, sipping her punch, not trusting herself to ask any questions without choking up. Her commitment to noncommitment had disappeared long before the end of the meeting.

Jesselene soon sat down beside Elizabeth. "What did you think of the speakers, dear?" Jesselene asked.

"They were wonderful—especially you."

Jesselene blushed. "I think I got a little carried away," she said.

"No, it was perfect," Elizabeth said.

"Does that mean you want to help?" she asked.

"I think so," Elizabeth said. "I really do." Unbidden, the insecurity returned. "But will you help me until I know what I'm doing?"

"Of course I will. We'll learn together." She opened a pocket calendar she was carrying, and they looked over the schedule together. Elizabeth soon picked two evenings during the next two weeks to come in to help. Then someone called Jesselene from across the room. But before she left, a mischievous look crossed her face. "Don't eat your doughnut," she said. "I was too nervous to eat anything before I left home, and I'm starving. Let's go get a pizza to eat after we finish here. Okay?"

Elizabeth quickly wrapped the doughnut in a napkin for Megan's breakfast. "I'd love to," she said. "I'll give Paul a call."

"Great." Then she was gone, wending her way across the room, talking excitedly and spreading enthusiasm as she went, leaving Elizabeth to sit and wonder in her wake why she had chosen her to share a pizza with.

• • •

Jesselene felt cozy sitting in the dim restaurant waiting for their pizza. Elizabeth was not very talkative as she sipped her water and fingered her napkin, so Jesselene chattered away, entertaining her with funny and interesting stories about the women who were at the meeting that night. Then she told stories about her children when they were young. By the time the pizza had come, Elizabeth was laughing and pressing her for more stories.

"Okay," she agreed. "But only if you'll tell me about yourself while I eat a piece of pizza. Speaking in front of a crowd always makes me hungry."

The darkness of the room concealed Elizabeth's eyes, but Jesselene could hear the regret in Elizabeth's voice as she spoke quietly. "My life hasn't been nearly as interesting as yours," she said.

"Let me decide that," Jesselene replied. "Tell me how you met your husband. Paul, right?"

Elizabeth nodded. So, beginning with meeting Paul in college, she told her about struggling through law school, tight budgets, and small apartments until Paul landed his present job and they bought their home.

A lot of it reminded Jesselene of the experiences she and Rowland had endured early in their marriage. "It was a wonderful story," Jesselene said. "Do you have family nearby?"

"Just Paul's," was all Elizabeth said.

"What a shame for your family to miss out on that sweet baby," Jesselene said, reaching for the check.

Elizabeth didn't respond to her observation but insisted on paying the bill herself. They finally agreed to split it.

"But only if you'll be my guest next time," Jesselene said. "And I really want there to be a next time."

"Oh," Elizabeth said, "I do too. I've had a nice time. Your family sounds wonderful."

They walked together to their cars, Jesselene's arm companionably tucked through Elizabeth's. It was just a natural extension of the warmth Jesselene felt with Elizabeth. What a splendid young woman, she thought. She needs to be a Mormon. But didn't everyone? Maybe she could invite Elizabeth and Paul and their darling baby over for dinner one night and fix some of her ward-famous lasagna. Diane would like Elizabeth. Elizabeth had a pretty smile just like Diane's and practically the same color of soft brown hair.

"If I thought you wouldn't mind spending an evening with us older folks, I'd invite you over for dinner," Jesselene said.

"We'd love it," Elizabeth answered. "I'd love to meet the children and husband who so willingly share you with others."

"You're too kind," Jesselene said.

She watched from her car as Elizabeth drove away. She should have talked about the church instead of rambling on about her family, but she hadn't felt really impressed to. Maybe that would come later. As she started the engine, she wondered about Elizabeth. Usually she was fairly accurate on first impressions, and she had the definite feeling that Elizabeth was much more complicated than she appeared on the surface. She had finally gotten Elizabeth to loosen up and laugh, but even then a touch of loneliness seemed to cling to her.

She knew she wanted to see Elizabeth again. Rowland would say that she was just being drawn to another woman of that age, but she wasn't. She really liked Elizabeth. Besides, Elizabeth couldn't possibly be more than twenty-three or twenty-four. At least four years too young.

8

Saturday evening came quickly. Paul still had not brought up the subject of a religious video being shown at the Robertson home. Even as eloquent as he was at times in the courtroom, words failed him when it came to convincing Bets that religion could be an important part of life. It took him until they pulled up in front of the Robertsons to think of anything remotely casual enough. "Bets?" he finally said.

"Yes?" She unbuckled Megan.

"If the Robertsons say anything about their church, you won't mind, will you?"

She looked at him suspiciously. "Why would you ask that?"

"No real reason," he said.

"Don't worry, honey," she said. "They invited us over for dinner, that's all." She lifted Megan onto her lap and opened the car door, not really paying much attention to him. "But even if they want to, I'll be good."

He knew that he really hadn't prepared her yet for the video. But since Nephi and Jeanine, followed by a parade of children, were walking down the sidewalk to welcome them, he didn't have much choice but to get out. Maybe he could find a moment inside to tell her.

"Your home is lovely," Elizabeth said as they walked in. She had assumed that a home housing so many children would have to resemble a large toybox.

Jeanine laughed. "Thank the children. I was after them all day to keep their things out of the living room and dining room. I don't have the nerve to see what their bedrooms look like."

A buzzer called Jeanine to the kitchen, so Elizabeth followed Paul and Nephi into a comfortable den. She put Megan down on the floor in the middle of a pile of toys with Sarah. Paul immediately noticed the computer system that covered a large desk along one wall, and soon Nephi and Paul were engrossed in conversation about software programs and hardware. Elizabeth wandered around the rest of the room as she kept an eye on the babies.

Every picture in the room seemed to be handmade cross-stitchings. How Jeanine had time to do something like that was beyond Elizabeth. She had started some kind of handwork one time, but it had wound up hopelessly knotted. She hadn't even thought about anything like that since Megan had been born. Maybe Jeanine could untangle her picture and help her—she certainly seemed to be talented in that direction.

Several were sayings with pictures of flowers or children. "Love spoken here"—she loved that one. "Families are forever." Paul had said something about their belief in that. "I am a child of God." Interesting.

A voice at her shoulder said, "My talented wife did all these." She turned to see Nephi behind her.

"They're beautiful," Elizabeth said.

Paul joined them. "Maybe Jeanine could help you untangle that one you started, Bets."

Her response to that uncalled-for remark was a withering

glance. "I think I'll go help Jeanine. Can you watch Megan?"

"Sure," he said humbly.

She found Jeanine putting a huge pan of enchiladas on the table. "Those look delicious," she said.

"Thanks. I thought everyone could just fill their plates. I'll put the children at the table, and we adults can sit out in the living room. Our table has sort of outgrown us and company."

"That's fine." She followed Jeanine into the kitchen where Jeanine sprinkled lettuce over what looked to be a taco salad. "Where did you learn to cook Mexican food?"

"Oh," Jeanine answered, "when I was a teenager my father was a mission president in Mexico for our church, and we got to know a lot of good cooks. It was sort of a hobby for my mother and me."

Elizabeth didn't know what a mission president was, but their church seemed to be in every part of their life—even their food. It had to get tiresome.

Dinner was delicious, and conversation about work and children flowed easily. Paul loved the enchiladas so much that, after the dishes were scraped and stacked, Jeanine sat Elizabeth down with a stack of note cards to copy down all her Mexican recipes. "If I'm not careful, I'm going to get inspired by all your homemaking skills," Elizabeth joked.

"Don't be silly," Jeanine said. "I was just an only daughter, and my mother made sure I was taught well."

"You're lucky you had a good mother to teach you things like that," Elizabeth said.

"Yes, I am."

Elizabeth looked up from copying the recipes as the two men came back into the living room. Nephi was holding a videotape in his hand, and Paul was standing behind him, looking a little pasty. Maybe the enchiladas weren't setting well with him, Elizabeth thought.

"Elizabeth," Nephi said. "Paul said he'd be interested in seeing a tape we have about our church and families. Would you mind?"

She understood now. It wasn't the enchiladas—it was the conversation they had had out in front of the house in the car. Paul smiled weakly at her and shrugged his shoulders just enough for her to notice.

"No, I don't mind," she answered. It certainly didn't matter one way or the other to her life what their video was about.

As the video started a few minutes later in the den, Paul sat next to Elizabeth on the couch. He leaned forward as if he didn't want to miss a word, but Elizabeth sat back, wishing that Megan would start screaming uncontrollably so she'd have a good excuse to leave after a few minutes. At the moment, though, it looked as if Megan were totally content sucking on a vanilla wafer.

A little over an hour later, the Danforths bid good-bye for the evening. The trip home began in silence. Even Megan settled down into her car seat and fell asleep without a whimper. Paul seemed miles away from Elizabeth as she watched the lights go by.

Finally, about halfway home, Paul put his arm on the back of the seat and touched Elizabeth gently on the shoulder. "Bets?"

"What?"

"Wouldn't you like this to be true?"

"My wanting it to be true doesn't make it so."

"You're right." He was quiet a minute. "But why can't you believe that God loves us and wants us to be happy?"

"Who is the 'us'?"

"Everyone—his children."

She was silent for a long time. They were almost home when she finally spoke, quietly but with conviction. "I used to want to believe that God loved me. But where was his love all those nights I cried for a family, my own family? Where was his love when my mother—whoever she is—gave up her own child?"

"But she thought she was giving you to a family who would love you."

"So where was God when they were killed three months later?"

It was Paul's turn to be silent for a while. After some time, he said, "I don't know, Bets. I don't know why your life was like that, but I do believe God loves you. Maybe you should give him another chance."

They had stopped in the driveway. "Maybe I should," she said. "And maybe one day my long-lost parents will show up at our doorstep with armfuls of presents for their daughter."

They left their conversation behind them in the car as they got out. The night ended in silence for both of them.

• • •

The rest of Sunday after mass was quiet. Paul didn't mention the Church again, not wanting to diminish the feeling he had had since the video the night before by talking to Bets about it. After dinner, he settled down for a football game while Bets bundled Megan up for a walk. Usually she begged him to go with them, but today she didn't.

After they left, Paul thought about Nephi telling him that they could come over and meet the missionaries anytime he felt as if he were ready. Or he could go to church with them.

He'd like to, but how would he convince Bets to go along with it? He felt that this should be a family thing. Every part of the Robertsons' life seemed to be touched by their church, so how could he leave the most important part of his life—Bets—out of it?

While he was contemplating that, the phone rang. It was Nephi.

"Hi, Paul," he said. "I was just sitting here thinking about you and Elizabeth and thought I'd call to see how she handled last night. Was she upset?"

Paul was glad to hear his voice. "No, not really, I guess. We talked about it some last night, but she wasn't really mad." He thought a second, wondering how to describe Bets's reaction. "More like she was worried, I think."

"Worried?"

"That I'm taking this too seriously, I suppose."

"Well, are you?"

"Yes, I am," Paul said. It felt good to put it into words. "I've never really had a feeling like this before, or such curiosity about anything." Then a hint of regret crept into his voice. "I just wish Bets shared my interest in your church. I've known since I first met her that she has an aversion to religion, but until now it hasn't mattered that much."

"Give her some time," Nephi said. "All of us are in different stages of spiritual growth. We can go just as slowly as she needs to."

But she doesn't want to go anywhere, Paul thought.

"The gospel is meant to bring happiness," Nephi continued. "When she understands that, maybe she'll be more receptive."

"Yeah, maybe." But as they continued to talk, a sudden desire to be with Bets and Megan came to Paul. He was sure Nephi was right—if Bets could see that this gospel of Nephi's could only bring them happiness, then surely she would listen with him. "Thanks for calling, Nephi. I think I'll go find her and spend some time with Megan and her."

"Great," Nephi said. "I'll see you at work tomorrow, and we can talk more if you want."

After Paul hung up, he ran to the closet to grab his jacket, then rushed through the front door. He stood for a minute on the front porch breathing in the crispness of the air, his heart full of gratitude to someone for something that remained beyond his ability to define. But there was a promise in the air he felt as he jogged easily down the street, filled with the anticipation of seeing Bets and Megan and assured that the future could bring the happiness that Bets had sought for so long. He knew he could convince her. He had to, however long it took.

CHAPTER

9

The happiness of the evening before remained with Elizabeth as she squeezed in a few minutes of shopping before she met Carla for lunch. Paul had been overjoyed when he met them in the park, grabbing her in a big hug, then kissing and tickling Megan while she squirmed and giggled. They had had a leisurely walk in the park, followed by a long wonderful evening in front of the den fire. She hoped to continue that feeling with a special dinner tonight.

Paul had been so relaxed and content, not mentioning that church a single time. She was sure that he had decided to forget about Nephi and Jeanine's church, and everything would be perfect again.

After shopping, while Elizabeth waited for Carla in one of the popular downtown restaurants, she wondered why Carla had called and asked to meet her for lunch. When Elizabeth worked full-time before Megan was born, they had met for lunch frequently. Since Elizabeth had quit work, though, they hadn't seen much of each other. Actually, that hadn't bothered her because Carla was a little overbearing at times, and Elizabeth had a feeling that Carla found her a little boring since she had chosen to stay home with Megan. Carla made it clear that she never regretted not having children. Elizabeth saw her come in the door, dressed beautifully, of course. Carla owned the most fashionable — and expensive — dress shop in town.

"Hi, sweetie," Carla said, brushing Elizabeth's cheek with a kiss. She slid into a chair and pulled out her trademark cigarette.

"Hi," Elizabeth said. "How's the dress shop business?"

"Great! Why don't you stop by, and I'll show you some of the new fall fashions?"

Elizabeth wondered if that was a comment on her appearance.

"So how's that baby?" Carla said.

"Beautiful." She shared a couple of stories about Megan, and Carla at least acted as if she were interested.

Lunch proceeded pleasantly enough, and Elizabeth had to admit to herself that Carla kept her entertained with all the news — more like gossip — of the people in the law firm. About dessert time, Carla finally got around to the subject of Jeanine. "I had lunch with her last week, you know," she said.

"No, I didn't," Elizabeth said. She couldn't imagine Carla and Jeanine being lunch pals.

"Benjamin thought it would be good for the firm to make her feel welcome, so being the obedient wife that I am, I took her out to lunch." She laughed, then dived into her dessert.

"So — did you enjoy it?"

She shrugged. "It was all right. She wore the prettiest suit. If I had that many kids, I don't think I'd even get out of bed in the morning, much less get out of my bathrobe."

"She's really good with her children," Elizabeth said. She thought back to Jeanine's sparkling house and happy children. "She's a great cook too. We had the best meal over there the other night."

Carla raised her perfectly penciled eyebrows. "Now I'm surprised. Visiting at each other's home?"

"They're nice people." It was Elizabeth's turn to be surprised—she was defending the Robertsons. "Jeanine has done a beautiful job decorating their home. It's full of her needlework."

"My, I'm impressed," Carla said sarcastically. "Let me guess—you've decided to go for five children, too."

Suddenly Elizabeth was tired of her lunch date. She thought how much more she had enjoyed her dinner with the Robertsons, even with the video on religion. "Well, Carla, this has been real nice, but I have to be going. I've planned a special dinner for Paul tonight." She pushed the last of her dessert away, folding her napkin beside it.

"I need to be going, too," Carla said. "We're getting some new merchandise in this afternoon. Don't forget to stop by the shop." She looked up and smiled sweetly at Elizabeth. "You'd be amazed at what the right fall colors could do for your complexion."

"Thanks," Elizabeth said. "I'll try not to forget." Then, leaving Carla in her cloud of smoke, she thankfully escaped.

• • •

Jesselene dumped her shopping bags beside the chair and practically fell into it. Her feet knew that she had been shopping all morning. A few people had donated some money to TLC, so she had searched for good prices on car seats and cribsheets. Those two things always seemed to wear out by the time the babies stopped needing them. She pushed herself up a little straighter and looked around at the other tables. Usually, she didn't like eating by herself in a restaurant, but this particular one was famous for its chef salad and was one of her favorite places to eat.

As the waitress left to deliver her order, Jesselene marked off the things on her list that she had bought. As she put the list back into her purse, she glanced around the dining area again. Then she saw Elizabeth sitting across the room, with her back to Jesselene. The woman sitting with Elizabeth was talking and gesturing with her cigarette. Jesselene thought the woman's face was familiar, but it took her a few minutes to remember that she knew her from an ad in the paper for a boutique that Jesselene had ventured into only once.

She watched for a moment to see if Elizabeth picked up a cigarette, though she knew that it wasn't any business of hers. She was relieved, however, when she saw Elizabeth wave a cloud of smoke away from herself.

Contemplating Elizabeth's choice of lunch dates while she ate, Jesselene decided that Elizabeth must have a side to her that she hadn't seen if her friends came from the society page. Strange how you could think that you knew someone and then find out you really didn't. Maybe everyone had the right to some secrets in their life. Nobody in Waynesboro, except Rowland, knew everything about her past. Not even her children.

Elizabeth stood up from the table, but her friend didn't seem to be moving. Jesselene tucked her head down and concentrated on her cucumbers in case Elizabeth wanted to go on by and pretend she didn't see her.

"Jesselene," Elizabeth said. "I just saw you. Have you been here long?"

"Oh, hello, Elizabeth." Jesselene wiped her mouth and hoped she didn't smell like ranch dressing. "I've been here a while. I saw you, but I didn't want to bother you and your friend."

Elizabeth shook her head. "I wouldn't call her that." She pulled a chair out. "Do you mind if I sit down?"

"I'd love for you to."

Elizabeth leaned over to whisper, "Can she see what I'm saying?"

"No." Jesselene smiled. "She's paying attention to something pink and frothy in a big glass."

"She's happy then."

Jesselene finished her salad while Elizabeth told her all about the wives of the law firm and the special dinner she was planning for Paul that night. "It sounds lovely, dear." She tucked her napkin under her plate. "And this has been nice, too, but I promised to pick up Steve at the high school and take him to the library, so I'd better be going."

"I'm glad I had a chance to talk with you," Elizabeth said. "I guess I'll see you Thursday night."

"You won't chicken out on me, will you?"

"No, I'm looking forward to it."

They strolled out together after Jesselene paid her bill. Their cars were parked about a block apart, so Jesselene watched as Elizabeth walked away from her. Maybe she was wrong, but she thought that she had just seen the real Elizabeth — one her friend Carla didn't know.

She wondered as she headed for the station wagon if she could ever be as sure about the real Jesselene. Was her whole life just an attempt to cover up the pain she still felt? Would she ever know?

• • •

Elizabeth had read through an entire magazine and started over before she saw the headlights of the Mercedes turn into the driveway. That was her cue to dash into the dining room and light the candles on the table set for two. "Oh shoot," she said, trying keep the candles straight. The second candle flickered into a flame as he walked into the house.

"Bets, I'm home," he called.

"In here." She walked nonchalantly through to the kitchen door to meet him.

"Wow," he said. He stopped in the doorway to survey the dimly lighted room. "What's the occasion? It sure smells good. Looks good too."

"I just thought I'd treat us to a special dinner," she said. "Is that okay?"

"That's great." He pulled a huge bouquet of flowers from behind his back. "I guess I was inspired to stop and get these, then."

"They're beautiful." She kissed him on the cheek, then brushed past him to find a vase. On TV the actress would reach right into the proper cabinet to pull out a crystal vase, then drop the flowers into it, immediately creating a beautiful arrangement. It took her three tries, though, to find a vase big enough, and even then her arrangement seemed a little lopsided.

Paul was peeking into one of the pots on the stove. "Is this spaghetti?" he asked. "I'm starved."

"It sure is. With mushrooms and ground sirloin." She took a big bowl from the refrigerator and placed it on the table. "And Caesar's salad and crescent rolls." She then put out the spaghetti noodles, sauce, and rolls.

"So what's the occasion?" he asked again, settling down at the table and looking at the silverware and fine porcelain serving bowls.

"Nothing. Can't a wife just fix a delicious, romantic meal for her husband when she wants to?" She poured red wine into their goblets as he attacked his salad.

"Paul," she said, "we forgot the toast." Holding his wine glass out for him, she noticed that he hesitated a bit before taking the glass, then shrugged. "To my wonderful husband

and our wonderful marriage and a wonderful evening." She clinked her glass against his.

He laughed. "That was a wonderful toast."

"Wasn't it, though?" She emptied her wineglass, but he took only a sip from his before putting down his glass and digging into his dinner again.

Everything was delicious, but even though Paul ate a huge dinner, he drank only one glass of wine. When they had finished, Elizabeth stood up and started clearing the table. "I'll get the dessert and take it out to the den," she said.

"Oh," he groaned, "just give me a little — I'm stuffed."

When she returned with two slices of cheesecake, he was standing facing the fire with his back to her. His hands were in his pockets as he gazed into the flames. "Paul?" she asked.

"What?" He turned around. "Oh, sorry, were you talking to me?"

"What were you thinking about?"

"Oh, nothing much." He followed her over to the couch where she patted the cushion beside her. He sat down, but his mind seemed elsewhere as he began to distractedly eat the cheesecake. After a few bites, he deliberately placed his cheesecake on the arm of the couch and swallowed. "Bets," he said, turning to her and clearing his throat, "I need to talk to you."

"Sure, honey." The intensity in his eyes was so unsettling that she looked down and stared at her cheesecake. She nervously took a small bite. The atmosphere she had worked so hard to achieve was disappearing.

"I talked to Nephi today about his church."

The piece of delicious cheesecake seemed to turn into a lump in her throat. She didn't want to have this conversation.

"There's no reason to get upset about this, Bets, but I want to know more about the Mormon religion."

"I don't," she said.

"Maybe if you just gave it a chance, you would."

He had done it. After all these years, he had stepped over the line so carefully and silently understood between them.

"Paul," she said miserably.

"I know you've never felt a need for a church or a religion, Bets, but I do, and I just have this feeling within me that Nephi and Jeanine have something that we need to have. It's hard to explain, but it's there."

"But I don't feel the need."

"You might if you let yourself. Nephi said the Church could help you so much."

She turned to him angrily. "So you've discussed your pitiful wife with him?"

"No," he defended himself. "Not really. He just wanted to know how you felt about the church video."

"How was I supposed to feel?" She stood up and walked over to the fire some distance away from him. "You dragged me over for dinner and conveniently forgot to tell me that were being treated to an evening of religion."

"You're exaggerating, Elizabeth." He didn't often call her Elizabeth. "And I apologize for that—I should have told you."

"Would it have made a difference?"

"I wanted to see the video."

"I didn't."

"You made that obvious." He was still sitting, staring up at her as she stared down at him. It had been a long time since they had had an argument. "Let's not argue, Bets. Maybe it won't come to anything. I just want to be able to ask some questions and find out more about the Mormon religion."

Elizabeth looked at the fire but didn't say anything.

"There is still freedom of religion, isn't there?"

"Don't start being a lawyer," she retorted.

"Isn't there anything about the Robertsons and the tape we saw that appeals to you?"

She gave the question a quick thought but couldn't come up with anything appealing that she would ever admit. "Nope," she said. What should she say? Her wonderful evening was ruined. She was afraid to ask him what his holy quest would involve, and if she did ask, maybe he'd think that she was giving her approval. She didn't want to do that, but insisting that he drop the whole issue wouldn't do any good either. Besides, she had never opposed him in anything that he wanted to do. She had never felt she had that right, and until now, she had never had the desire to. Finally she asked, "So what is this search for truth going to involve?"

"Well, Nephi said that he could bring me some things to read or we could go to church with them. Or we could go over to their house, and the missionaries could teach us some lessons about the Church. Or the missionaries could come to our house."

"Us? Our?"

"I was hoping that you'd go with me."

"Paul, there are just some people in the world who don't feel a need to belong to a church and worship the same way as everyone else. Can't you believe that this just might not be for me?"

"Can't you try to be even a little open-minded?"

"Now you're criticizing me," she said. She knew that Paul hated it when she accused him of that because he tried to be accepting and loving.

"But, sweetheart, if it's true for me and the Robertsons, and if we are children of God, and if God does have an overall plan for us, then it's true for all people. Truth is truth."

The picture that she had seen at the Robertsons came into her mind—I am a child of God. Suddenly weary, she rubbed her temples as he stood up and came over to stand beside her.

"Bets, I know how you've always felt, and I know that you have feelings from your childhood that you have a hard time getting rid of, but maybe it's time to try to let them go. Maybe it's time that you stop punishing God and give him a chance to love you."

Punishing God? So that was how he saw it. She had thought that, through all these years, he had been so understanding. He had paid for her to go see that psychotherapist who hadn't helped a bit. Yet all that time he had thought it all boiled down to a problem with religion. She had made a deal with God years ago—didn't they do that in the Bible too?—and so far he hadn't kept his part of the deal. He hadn't given her a family, so evidently he didn't want her faith.

Paul was talking again, "Will you just come with me, Bets? Even if you're not interested, could you just come with me to meet the missionaries?" He moved closer and drew her into his arms.

A part of her wanted to pull away and say no, she would never go. But the bigger part of her wanted to hide herself in his arms where she had always felt so much security and love. So she stayed. "I won't give you any guarantees," she said.

"I won't ask for any."

They stood together as the fire burned, miles apart yet so close there was no room for anger between them. They stood there until they heard Megan crying upstairs, then Elizabeth pulled away.

"I'll go," Paul said.

"No, I'll go," she said. "I'm exhausted. I'll go lie down with her."

He held onto her hand for as long as he could, until finally she let go and left him still standing by the fire and looking at her with a strangely peaceful look on his face. She supposed that he felt as if he had won, but she felt nothing—no anger, no peace, just exhaustion as she climbed the stairs to Megan.

CHAPTER

10

For the next two days, neither Paul nor Elizabeth mentioned the Church. Things were almost what Elizabeth considered to be normal, except that she sensed a certain enthusiasm about Paul that she hadn't seen before. Then one morning, as she looked for stamps in his desk, she found a book called the Book of Mormon and several pamphlets, which she didn't bother to open before tossing them back into the drawer.

By the time Thursday evening came — her first night at TLC — she had successfully pushed the Mormons from her thoughts. Paul had promised before he left for work that morning that he would be home in plenty of time for her to leave, but, as it turned out, he was late and barely had time to kiss her hello and apologize before kissing her good-bye. She was too excited to be mad at him and too nervous to do anything more than hand him Megan and point him toward dinner.

Most of her excitement had turned to apprehension by the time she reached the outside door of the office. She knew Jesselene was already there because she had parked next to her station wagon. In fact, their cars were the only two there, which she had been relieved to see. Maybe she would have a chance to feel more familiar with her responsibilities before she was called upon to exercise them.

The door to the Jesselene's inner office was open. "Knock, knock," she said. She could see Jesselene bent over the desk.

Jesselene looked up and smiled when she saw who it was. "Well, hello, Elizabeth. I didn't hear you come in. I guess I'm not very vigilant, am I?"

"Actually, I sort of snuck in, in case you were with someone," Elizabeth confessed.

"No, it's been quiet this evening so far." She sat back down and motioned for Elizabeth to take the rocking chair.

They chatted for a few minutes, with Jesselene filling her in on some changes they had made the past week to make things run more smoothly. That finished, Jesselene suddenly sat back in her chair and looked intently at Elizabeth.

Elizabeth looked back at her for a while, but then began to feel uncomfortable, so she smiled. "Is something wrong?"

"I was just going to ask you that," she said. "You look worried about something. Is everything okay at home? Megan isn't sick again, is she?"

"She's fine." Was it obvious that she was worried about Paul? She hadn't even thought much about it today because she had been getting ready to come here. Elizabeth considered briefly telling her about Paul's sudden interest in the Mormons, but she didn't have a chance to decide as they heard the outer door open, then close. Elizabeth jumped up and looked desperately at Jesselene. "What do we do?" she asked.

"First of all, calm down," Jesselene said, laughing. "Let's go see who it is. And don't worry, I'll handle it."

They walked out together, Jesselene with her arm around

Elizabeth. Elizabeth pasted what she hoped was a reassuring smile on her face.

"May we help you, dear?" Jesselene said to the young woman in front of them. She sounded so calm and efficient.

"Yes, may we help you?" Elizabeth echoed. It sounded better when Jesselene had said it.

"My friend told me that you had baby formula," the woman said. "I'm . . . I'm sort of short of money until the end of the week, and my baby is out of formula."

"Well, your friend was right. We have lots of formula."

Jesselene put her arm around Elizabeth again. "Why doesn't Elizabeth get some for you, and we can go into the office to talk. We'd like to have some information about you and your baby, if you don't mind. It isn't required if you'd rather not — but we'd like to make sure you're getting all the help you're entitled to. Is that okay?"

"That's fine," the woman said. Jesselene seemed to have put her at ease immediately, and the woman followed her down the hall. Only Elizabeth was still nervous. She stood in the middle of the room and tried to remember where the formula was. As she stood wondering and feeling very stupid, Elizabeth saw Jesselene stick her head back into the room. "It's in the storage area at the end of the hallway," Jesselene whispered, "left-hand cupboard."

The formula was right where Jesselene said it would be — right where she had shown Elizabeth during the training session. With shaking hands, Elizabeth took out a large can and even remembered to include a sheet containing mixing instructions and tips on infant nutrition. She felt much calmer as she walked back toward the office. She had actually helped someone. Her feeling of elation lasted all the way down the hall until she saw another young and very pregnant woman standing just inside the door, looking lost.

Glancing into the office, she saw that Jesselene was still busy with the first woman. It was up to her. "I'll be right with you," she said to the woman. She placed the formula inside the office door. "There's someone else here," she whispered to Jesselene as she looked up from the papers she was filling out.

"Can you handle it, hon'?" Jesselene asked. "I'll be finished in a minute."

"I'll try."

"You'll do fine." Jesselene smiled confidently.

The woman was still huddled by the door. The thought crossed Elizabeth's mind that maybe she was in labor and that delivery was only moments away. She steeled herself for whatever might lie ahead and forced herself to look calm. "Hi," she said. "I'm Elizabeth. What may I help you with tonight?"

"I need some clothes," the woman said.

"Good. Why don't you come and sit down where you'll be more comfortable?"

The woman reluctantly followed Elizabeth over to the couch, where she sat down and huddled in the corner. Elizabeth sat in the rocking chair beside her.

"May I ask your name?" Elizabeth asked.

"Claudia," the woman answered.

"Well, Claudia," Elizabeth said, feeling more and more confident. "You said you needed clothes. Do you need clothes for yourself or for your baby?"

"My baby."

"When is your baby due?" It couldn't be too long.

"Next week."

"That's exciting," Elizabeth said. "I have a baby girl."

"You do?"

Elizabeth nodded her head. "So you need some clothes for the baby to wear after you bring it home?"

"Yes, ma'am."

"Have you been going to the doctor regularly?"

"Yes, ma'am."

"Good." Elizabeth stood up, smiling down at Claudia, who had visibly relaxed. "Why don't you follow me into the back, Claudia, and I'm sure we can pick out some nice clothes to bring that baby home in."

They went into the back room, and in a few minutes, they were chatting happily about babies and soft little stretch suits. Elizabeth found out through the conversation that Claudia was married to a young man who was temporarily out of work because of surgery.

"But as soon as he's back to work, we'll be able to take care of our baby just fine," she assured Elizabeth.

"I'm sure you will," Elizabeth said, at once feeling very motherly and relieved.

Jesselene poked her head in the door after a few minutes. "Everything okay?"

"Just fine." Elizabeth smiled. "But maybe you can talk to Claudia after she picks out some more clothes to see if we can help her in any other way."

"Be glad to," Jesselene said. "Just bring her by the office before she leaves." And she left them alone wondering over the size of the tiny booties Claudia was holding.

● ● ●

"So, what do you think?" Jesselene asked Elizabeth. They had locked up and were straightening the waiting room, which really hadn't even gotten messed up.

"I liked it," Elizabeth said. "It was such a good feeling helping those women."

"And you were so good at it. You put that one girl right at ease."

Elizabeth smiled. "I really didn't think I could do it."

"You were great. I don't think you even need me."

Elizabeth turned quickly from the pillows she was fluffing. "No. Don't you dare desert me. You promised."

"I know, hon'. I won't."

Elizabeth sighed with relief. "Well, maybe after next week I could do it by myself—for a little bit. Maybe."

They walked out to their cars together.

Elizabeth laughed. "I feel so different than when I came in. I was so nervous at first, but now I feel great."

"You don't have that worried look you had around your eyes when you came in either," Jesselene said.

That was the first time Elizabeth had even thought about Paul and his Mormon project since she had arrived at TLC. But even being reminded about it didn't spoil the contented feeling she had, and the thought of confiding in Jesselene didn't reenter her mind. "It was fun," she said. "I guess I'll see you next week."

"I'll be here," Jesselene said. She waved good-bye as she climbed into her car.

Elizabeth drove home quickly, anxious to report to Paul about her evening. She couldn't believe that she hadn't even thought to call home to check if everything was all right.

She found him in the study, reading from a thick, legal-looking book. Beside that was the Book of Mormon she had seen in his drawer, but she decided to ignore it. "Hi, I'm home." She grabbed him around his neck and kissed him.

Paul smiled. "How'd it go? I thought you'd call me."

"It was great. We were so busy I didn't get a chance to call. Is Megan okay?"

"Of course. So, what did you do?"

She told him—every little detail that she could remember.

When she finished, he smiled again. "I'm glad you enjoyed it."

"Me, too," she said. "In fact, I think I'll go make us some hot chocolate to celebrate."

"Okay." Before she could leave, he grabbed her hand and looked as if he were about to say something.

She waited expectantly, but he didn't. "Want something else?" she asked.

"No," he said slowly, letting go of her hand.

She left the room, but, glancing back at him from the hallway, she saw him put the Book of Mormon back into the drawer and close it softly, almost sadly.

Maybe I should have talked to Jesselene, she thought as she took the chocolate down. But why spoil a good evening and even think about it? She had a feeling that there would be plenty of opportunities to talk to Paul about the Mormons. But tonight belonged to her and TLC.

11

The next morning, Paul looked his reflection in the eyes as he tied his necktie, pretending that he was talking to Bets. "Bets, guess what? We're going over to the Robertsons' tomorrow night to meet the missionaries." Then she would say, "I'd love to, honey. What time?"

No such luck. Maybe more humility would help. "Bets, is it all right if I tell Nephi that we could come over to their house tomorrow night and talk to the Mormon missionaries?" No, she always said that she admired his forcefulness and self-confidence in court.

The truth—he'd try the truth. After all, this is what the whole thing was about anyway. Truth. And he knew he'd found it. He'd read almost the entire Book of Mormon this past week, and its truthfulness jumped up from the pages at him as if the words were alive. If Bets would just start reading it, he was sure that she couldn't deny it.

One step at a time, though, he thought. He gave his tie one last jerk, then slipped on his coat. It was time to talk to the real Bets.

Bets was still talking excitedly about her evening at

TLC, and not until he had almost finished his breakfast did he have a chance to get a word in. "Remember when I said that I might want to meet the Mormon missionaries?"

"Yes." She kept her back turned to him as she stacked the dishes.

"Would tomorrow night suit you to go over to Nephi and Jeanine's?"

"Paul." She turned around and, leaning back against the sink, looked at him. "I don't see why you want me to go. I'm just not interested."

"But I want you to be with me."

Silence.

"Just come with me, and we'll find out together."

"Find out what?"

"Whether or not this is true."

She turned to face him then and looked truly puzzled. "But what if I don't care if it is or not?"

It was his turn to look puzzled. "Why wouldn't you? If it is true, then it's the whole purpose of life."

"You're losing me, Paul. I don't think everyone's purpose in life is the same."

"I mean generally speaking. Like the things you need to learn and do so you can live with God again after you die."

"So I'm going to hell if I don't go to the Robertsons'?"

"I didn't say that. They don't believe that, anyway."

She sounded irritated. "Are you an authority now on what the Mormons believe?"

He tried to ignore her cattiness. "I've been reading a lot this week. But do we have to argue? Can't you just go with me and see?"

"I don't want to. Why don't you just forget this, okay? We were perfectly happy before the Robertsons showed up. Go talk to your priest about this."

"I don't need to talk to the priest—I need my wife to be a little more open-minded."

"I am open-minded. I feel the same way about all churches."

Paul sighed and glanced at his watch. He was going to be late if he didn't leave soon. "Can we talk about it tonight? Will you just think about going tomorrow night?"

"I don't know, Paul. I just don't know."

An idea popped into his mind, and he opened his brief-case to pull out a couple of the pamphlets Nephi had brought him. "Here, Bets. Maybe if you read some of these today, you'll understand what I'm saying. Will you do that?" He held them out, but when she made no attempt to take them from him, he laid them on the table. "Do it for me, please?"

The look on her face was not encouraging. When he reached over to kiss her good-bye, she responded with a half-hearted kiss. He didn't like to leave with the situation the way it was, but he was really pushing the clock now. He looked at her, hoping for some sign that she would at least consider reading the material, but he couldn't see one on her face. "I love you, Bets. Bye-bye, Megan." He closed the door softly behind him.

● ● ●

Elizabeth listened to the sound of Paul's car backing out of the driveway, then looked over with a heavy heart at the babbling baby. If anyone had told her one month ago that her biggest concern would be that her husband would want to become a Mormon, she would have told them they were crazy.

She gave Megan her juice cup. "I love your daddy," she told her. "But why does he want to do this?" Megan smiled at her before grabbing the cup, but Elizabeth couldn't read anything from that, as hard as she tried. She pushed her cup of instant coffee away because she had lost her appetite even for that. "I don't even like the stuff," she told Megan. "Yucky, yucky," she said while making an ugly face, and Megan laughed.

"Mommy's funny, huh?" Elizabeth wiped Megan's hands with a napkin, pulling off the little pieces that stuck to her sticky fingers. "Okay, little girl, let's go see what kind of a day we have to work with. Maybe we'll just take off and spend the day at the park."

They stared out the back door at the pouring rain. "Maybe we won't." She nuzzled the softness of Megan's neck, wishing that everything was as simple and enjoyable as loving her baby. "Why can't I be like them?" she asked, continuing to look at the rain. "Why does this religion thing come so easily to others and so hard to me? Why can't I want to know about the Mormons? I don't even know if I want to want to know."

That last statement must have boggled Megan's imagination because she grabbed Elizabeth's nose and dug her sharp little fingernails in.

"Okay, okay, no more questions," Elizabeth said, prying her nose free. Suddenly she brightened, even as the downpour increased. "I know what we can do. Let's go take some of your old baby clothes over to TLC and see Jesselene. This is her morning to work." Without even questioning her motives this particular morning, she bounced up the stairs with Megan giggling.

Packing a box full of cute and expensive pink and pastel baby clothes took nearly a full hour. Megan climbed all over her the whole time and struggled, successfully at times, to unpack the whole box.

Maybe I just shouldn't go to TLC, Elizabeth considered. Struggling with Megan had used up her patience and a lot of her energy — it would be easier to stay home, put Megan down for a nap. But she did want to see Jesselene, and maybe the clothes she had packed would be needed this weekend. Okay, she'd go.

● ● ●

Jesselene was at the coffee table, sorting pamphlets on infant and child care, when Elizabeth and Megan came through the door. Megan was screaming in Elizabeth's arms as Elizabeth struggled to hold onto the box and the baby. Elizabeth's hood had fallen away from her face and her hair hung in wet ringlets, dripping down her raincoat into a puddle at her feet. She dropped the box inside the door with a thud.

"Elizabeth," Jesselene said, rushing over to them. "You're dripping wet. What's wrong with the baby?" She took Megan from Elizabeth.

Elizabeth pulled off Megan's cape as quickly as she could. "She's scared to death of this rain cape, for some reason."

"Poor baby," Jesselene said. She cradled Megan's head against her shoulder as Megan began to calm down. "Let's go see if we can find Mommy a towel before she catches her death of cold."

They were back soon with a baby towel and a calmer Megan. As Elizabeth dried herself off, Jesselene handed Megan a rattle to chew on and settled down in the rocking chair. "What brings you all out on a dreadful day like today?" Jesselene asked.

"It seems sort of silly now," Elizabeth said. "We came to bring you these clothes, but we should have waited for a better day, I guess."

"Aren't you sweet?" Jesselene said. Megan had fallen asleep in her arms, still giving an occasional sob. Jesselene laid her gently on the couch, propping pillows beside her to keep her from falling off, then covered her with one of the afghans. Picking up another afghan, she turned to Elizabeth. "Here, dear," she said. "Put this afghan around you and sit down. I'll go turn the thermostat up so you won't catch a chill."

"I'm fine, really," Elizabeth said to her as Jesselene disappeared down the hall.

"Don't you just love cozy, rainy days?" Jesselene asked when she returned. "A perfect day for staying home and cuddling a sweet baby." She patted Megan before she sat down. It seemed like ages ago since she had patted her own babies to sleep. "So why did you decide to come out—I would have dropped by to pick these up."

"That's okay," Elizabeth said. "I really wanted to get out of the house today and forget my troubles."

"So I was right," Jesselene said. "You do look sad— again."

Elizabeth wiped dripping mascara off her face. "I think it's just mascara."

"I know mascara and I know sad," Jesselene said firmly. "Is there anything I can help with?"

"No, I'll be okay," Elizabeth said.

"Are you sure?" Jesselene asked. "I'm a good listener."

"Oh, I'm sure you are," Elizabeth said. "It's just sort of complicated."

Jesselene waited. Megan was snoring little baby snores, and that was the only sound in the office.

"My husband and I are just having some problems," Elizabeth confided.

That certainly covered a wide variety of possibilities, Jesselene thought. "Oh, dear," she responded, "I do hope it's nothing serious. Such a beautiful baby needs a happy mommy and daddy."

"I know," Elizabeth sighed.

"But you know," Jesselene said, "marriages are never without challenges. Rowland and I still have some real lively arguments, and we've been married a lot longer than you have." Leaning over, she took Elizabeth's chilly hand in her own warm one.

"It's just that Paul wants to make some changes in our life that I'm not at all sure about." She sighed again. "I suppose it's actually nothing bad. And I'm sure some women would welcome the changes, but I don't. I just won't let myself."

Jesselene leaned back, folded her arms, and contemplated the worry on Elizabeth's face. "I don't know if this will help, but back when our children were younger, we had a problem that seems similar to the one I understand you're having."

"You did?" Her eyes widened with interest.

"Maybe," Jesselene said. "Rowland left one Saturday morning to get some worms to take our son Steven fishing. He came back a couple of hours later all excited with a huge, brand-new boat trailing behind the truck. He had bought the boat — without asking me — and decided that we would now be a boating family."

Elizabeth shook her head and smiled. "Did you chew him out?"

"Well, I let him know I sure wasn't pleased. To make a long story short, I spent the summer at home or watching from the shore, absolutely refusing to get on that boat while the rest of the family had a great time. Then one day toward the end of that long summer, it was such a beautiful day, and all the kids just begged and begged me to get on the boat. So I swallowed my pride, jumped on, and had a wonderful time. We stayed on that boat as long as we could that fall until we absolutely froze. And you know what?"

"What?"

"We later bought into a boating business, which we're still part-owners of after all these years." She laughed, remembering the past years.

"That's a good story," Elizabeth said.

"But did it help?" Jesselene asked.

"Maybe." She smiled, and the worried lines faded a bit from her forehead. "Maybe I'll just go buy a boat and spend the winter on it."

"Well, I know a good boating shop that would welcome your business." They both laughed merrily. Jesselene touched Elizabeth's hands again—they were now warm. "Now let's see these beautiful clothes you brought," Jesselene said.

"I really should go, I guess." She looked down at Megan, but she was still snoring.

"And wake that baby up?" Jesselene said. "Nonsense. I welcome the company." She sank down on the floor beside the box of clothes and gestured for Elizabeth to join her.

"Okay," Elizabeth said gratefully. And it seemed to Jesselene that her eyes had almost matched the smile on her lips.

● ● ●

Later at home, with Megan playing at her feet, Elizabeth thought back to her visit with Jesselene, feeling again the warmth that Jesselene seemed to bring into a room when she entered. She wondered if others felt it. Jesselene's children were certainly lucky to have such a strong family and wonderful mother. Maybe, she thought with a laugh, maybe they'd adopt her.

Her morning had worn her out, so she sank back against the couch pillows and reached behind her for the novel on the end table. The book she picked up, though, was the Book of Mormon that Paul had left beside her book that morning. She didn't immediately put it down as thoughts of boats weaved their way into her mind. A new boat would certainly have been easier to accept, but maybe she was being too hard on Paul. Maybe he could fit a new church into his life without letting it touch hers. He had been successful through the years with the Catholic church.

It wouldn't hurt to at least browse through the Book of Mormon to see why Paul felt it was so important. After all, what did she have to fear? One little plain black book was not going to change her life.

With her walls of defense strongly in place, she opened the book and began reading, "I, Nephi . . . " That explains Nephi's name, she thought. "Having been born of goodly parents . . . " See, nothing here for me. Even this Nephi person had parents.

12

Why, why, why, Paul thought to himself as he reluctantly rolled out of bed. Why did Megan always wake up before seven on the Saturday mornings it was his turn to get up with her, and why did she always sleep until at least nine on the Saturday mornings it was Bets's turn? Somehow on his next turn, he'd trick her on Friday night into thinking it was Bets's turn the next morning.

A few minutes and a dry Pampers later, he stumbled into the kitchen with Megan in his arms. For some reason — perhaps the early hour — he thought that he could station her on the floor and she'd stay put until he found the formula.

"Okay, Meggie baby," he said from within the refrigerator, "I know there was a can of formula in here last night. Here it is, babe." He pulled himself out of the fridge just as he noticed Megan next to him, giving a healthy baby tug on a full carton of eggs. A pool of broken eggs soon slid toward his naked feet.

"Oh, Megan," he cried. "How in the world did you do that?" He grabbed for her as she let go of the refrigerator and plopped down into the puddle of eggs. Half hopping across the floor, he deposited Megan into the left sink and hoisted himself up onto the counter to stick his foot into the right sink. He squeezed a generous amount of detergent into the water, which resulted in a generous amount of suds that filled his sink and delighted Megan, who was now sucking on the dishcloth.

"See the bubbles." Paul scooped up some in his hands and blew them at her. With a force that surprised him, she threw the dishcloth into the bubbles, sending them everywhere.

"Oh, baby," he said, "what will Mommy say if she comes down here and sees this mess we've made?" Thank goodness, Bets loved to sleep late.

"Say about what?" Bets asked. She came yawning into the kitchen, wrapping her robe around her. She looked over to see Megan in the sink, Paul with a foot stuck in the water, and bubbles dripping everywhere.

"Watch out, Bets," Paul called, not quite soon enough.

"Oh yuck," she said, looking down at her foot in the eggs. "What happened?"

"It was Megan."

She surveyed the kitchen as he spoke. "How can one grown man of above normal intelligence and one sweet little baby make such a horrible mess? You can't have been down here much longer than ten minutes."

"We're fast workers." He pointed to Megan, now covered with bubbles. "Really, it was all her fault."

"Blame it on the baby," she said. "Now don't move." Then she left the room. Sweeping back less than a minute later with towels in hand and Paul's bedroom slippers on her feet, she handed one towel to Paul and wrapped the baby in the other.

"Hey," Paul said, "those are my slippers."

"I'm not getting this mess on mine," she said. She

transferred Megan and a bottle into Paul's arms and none too gently pushed him toward the den.

He obeyed. He and Megan snuggled back into the couch to, as Paul hoped, catch a few more winks. Something, however, was digging into his back. Trying not to disturb the baby, who showed no signs of being the least bit sleepy, he reached behind him and felt for the offending object. Fully expecting it to be one of Bets's novels, which she frequently left on the couch cushions, he was surprised to find his copy of the Book of Mormon.

He contemplated it for a while, turning it over in his hands, trying to remember exactly where he had left the book and wondering if this meant that Bets had read even a little of it. Then he noticed the bookmark stuck on the page where the fifth chapter began. It was the bookmark one of his nieces had given Bets for Christmas last year, which she kept in whatever book she was reading. That Bets had read even one chapter, much less four, astounded him. He wondered about this new turn of events and how he could bring up the subject without doing any damage when Bets came back into the room, wiping her hands on a dishtowel.

"You owe me one," she said. "That was one of the worst messes I have ever cleaned up."

"I would have done it," he said humbly. He slid the Book of Mormon down behind him until he could think of a way to broach the subject.

Curling up in a chair, she closed her eyes.

Paul stared at her, trying to understand why she had suddenly begun to read the Book of Mormon. He was still staring at her when she shifted her position and opened her eyes. "Why are you staring at me?" she asked.

"Was I?"

"It looked like it." She closed her eyes again for a few

seconds, then teasingly opened them again to catch him in his stare. "See, you're staring."

"You're right," he admitted. A perfect opening. "I was wondering if you'd read any in the Book of Mormon I left you."

"What if I have?"

He pulled the book out from behind him. "I found your bookmark in it."

"You did?" she said.

"I just can't figure out why."

"You can't?" Then, just to frustrate him he knew, she closed her eyes again and sighed sleepily. Finally, unfolding herself from the chair, she stood over him and smiled down slyly. "I read it because you didn't bring home a boat. And it was okay—I didn't read much." Bets bent down and plucked Megan from his arms. He was left holding the half-empty bottle.

Boats? What did boats have to do with anything? He searched his memory, but nothing seemed to connect. "Boats?"

"I'll explain later. And," she paused, "if you want to go over to Nephi's, I won't fuss."

"You won't?" Couldn't he say anything that sounded halfway intelligent?

"But"—her tone of voice changed to determination— "I don't want anyone thinking that I'm interested in their church. Because I'm not." A nod of her head punctuated her statement, then she turned and disappeared up the stairs before he could answer her.

He had no idea why she had changed her mind. She might not be interested in the Mormon church, but she had decided to at least listen. It was going to be a great day. He looked at his watch. And it wasn't even seven-thirty yet.

· · ·

Everyone in the Robertsons' living room was having a relaxed, friendly evening — except Elizabeth, whose body lan-
guage read discomfort. She hadn't even meant to feel that
way when she had told Paul that she would come, but it
had turned out that way. Nephi and Jeanine were perfect
hosts, putting forth every effort to make their guests feel
welcome. Paul and Elizabeth were seated on a deep luxurious
couch, with the missionaries across from them in comfortable armchairs. A pile of toys awaited Megan's interest, and
Nephi and Jeanine were sitting on either side of the den
door where children kept popping their heads in from the
room in which they evidently were supposed to be entertaining themselves.

Elizabeth had planned on Megan crying when she was
put down in the strange room and disrupting the lessons so
that Elizabeth would be forced to leave, Megan clinging to
her shoulder. That way, she would miss the discussion. But,
when put down on the floor in front of the toys, Megan
grabbed up a Raggedy Ann and delightedly tried to pull the
doll's hair out. "I hope she doesn't bother anyone," Elizabeth
said hopefully.

"Oh, she'll be fine," Jeanine said. "If she gets unhappy,
I'll take her to the other room to play with the kids."

Oh no you won't, Elizabeth thought. I will.

The lesson began, with Paul leaning forward to hear
every word the missionaries said and Elizabeth focusing on
the hole in Elder Harrison's shoe. He was the skinny, dark-
haired missionary. The red-haired, freckled missionary who
didn't look old enough to shave, much less leave his mother
for longer than a school day, was Elder Thorne.

Nephi started with a prayer. So intently was Elizabeth
concentrating on Elder Harrison's shoe that she didn't re-
alize that she ought to bow her head until he had nearly

finished. Would Paul remember that she did not want them to ask her any questions? What if they asked her a question and she didn't know the answer? She was sure that she wouldn't know the answer because what she knew and believed about religion wouldn't fill the hole in Elder Harrison's shoe. She sat rigidly, hands folded together tightly and a smile frozen on her face. How could all these people in this room — except her — have faith? Where was she when it was handed out? Probably in some foster home. And why in the world was Megan so content to play for so long with that stupid Raggedy Ann?

She heard her name. Elder Thorne had asked her something. "Sister Danforth?" he questioned again. Her heart stopped.

Then Paul, her wonderful Paul, spoke up. Putting his arm around her and squeezing it reassuringly, he answered the missionary. "Elder Thorne," he said, "I'm the one who really wants to listen. My wife came along to give me moral support, so why don't you confine your questioning to me?"

The two missionaries exchanged a glance that Elizabeth thought was one of disappointment. "You bet," Elder Thorne said.

Elizabeth had never felt so in love with her husband as she did then. She reached over and took his hand, pressing it in gratitude. Then for the next few minutes, she closed her mind and heart completely to the conversation about happiness. But Paul was so interested in what they were saying that she didn't think he even remembered she was sitting beside him.

The lesson seemed endless, although, according to the clock she had been watching, only half an hour had passed. Elizabeth tried her best not to listen to what they were saying about death, sin, and atonement. These were pretty depressing subjects to start off with, she thought. Paul seemed particularly thrilled to hear what they had to say about prophets, even forgetting himself and looking over at Bets for her reaction. She smiled noncommittally for his sake, but prophets in this day and age seemed just a little farfetched. Then they started talking about the Book of Mormon. Suddenly the subject had become too familiar, and she felt that she had to get out of there. To her relief, Megan began fussing a little. She reached down into her bag and pulled out a diaper. Nobody ever tried to stop a woman leaving to change a baby's diaper.

"Excuse me," she whispered.

"We'll wait for you," Elder Harrison said brightly. She'd almost reached the door.

"It's okay," Paul said. "Let's just go on. She can catch up later if she wants to."

Elizabeth slipped into the kitchen and laid Megan over her lap to change her. She looked up to find that Jeanine had followed her out. A line of children in turn had followed Jeanine. They began patting and hugging Megan.

"You have the sweetest children," Elizabeth said sincerely.

"Thank you. They love babies. I guess it's from having so many of them around the house."

The women were silent for a few minutes, watching the children, then Jeanine looked at Elizabeth and spoke kindly, "You weren't very comfortable in there, were you?"

Elizabeth winced. "Was I that obvious?"

Jeanine smiled warmly.

"I'm sorry," Elizabeth said. She was surprised that Jeanine didn't seem to mind that she'd been uncomfortable — she had gotten the impression that they were very intense about their religion.

"Is it something I could help you with?" Jeanine asked. "Do you have any questions?" The two younger children came over to their mother and began tugging on her. Jeanine leaned over and picked up Julianne.

Elizabeth laid her cheek against the softness of Megan's hair, then smoothed the hair down again before she spoke. Speaking thoughtfully over the babble of the children was difficult, but she did. "That's just it, Jeanine. I have no questions because I'm just not interested in the Mormon church, or in any church for that matter." She watched, but Jeanine didn't seem to be thunderstruck.

"Do you know why?" Jeanine asked sincerely.

For a second, Elizabeth was tempted to spill the whole painful story of her childhood, but, with the noise of the children and the missionaries so close in the other room, it just didn't seem the appropriate time. In its place came a feeling that didn't come to Elizabeth very often, a feeling that she could share her life with the woman who sat across from her, that whatever she said would be taken into Jeanine's heart and given back to her in friendship.

"It's a long story," she said simply.

Jeanine looked intently at Elizabeth, as if she were listening to something inside of her, before asking, "Does it bother you that Paul is so interested in the Church?"

"That I haven't decided for sure yet," she said with a smile.

The quiet voices in the den changed to the distinct sound of men's laughter and an invitation from Nephi to follow him into the kitchen for refreshments. The lesson was over.

Jeanine moved, shaking children off of her, and came to stand before Elizabeth, kind understanding in her eyes. Elizabeth expected her to say something, but instead she embraced Elizabeth and Megan. "I think you and Paul will be just fine," she said. "And someday, when I'm not surrounded by a thousand children, I want to hear the long story."

The hug surprised Elizabeth. Before she could decide how she should reciprocate, Jeanine had released her and was at the counter handing down orders to children for napkins, cups, forks, and spoons.

Already noisy and busy, the kitchen became even noisier and busier when the men entered, deep in conversation.

"Do you know her? She's a member of the Church too," Nephi was saying.

"I didn't know that," Paul replied. "Did you hear that, Bets?"

Actually, it was hard to hear anything. "No, what?" she said.

"That Jesselene Manning you like so much is a Mormon too."

"Oh" was all Elizabeth could think to say. She'd gone her whole life without ever meeting a single Mormon that she knew of, and now they seemed to be everywhere. While everyone else sat or stood and sliced or scooped something, Elizabeth sat quietly and digested this news about Jesselene. It should make a difference in the way she felt about her, but it didn't seem to. She was just so thankful that she hadn't acted on the impulse to tell Jesselene about the problem she and Paul were having—it would have been so embarrassing to find out that she was a member of the church Elizabeth was fighting so much. She wondered what Jesselene would have said.

Her thoughts were interrupted by Elder Harrison sitting down beside her. "Is your baby okay?" he asked.

"She's fine."

"Great." He patted Megan's hand. "We'd like to invite you to come to church tomorrow. Your husband said he would like to come, and we'd like you to come, too."

Paul had left the room with Nephi, so Elizabeth couldn't tell if he had put the missionary up to this. "Thank you" was all she said. Ordinarily, she wouldn't have given such an invitation a second thought, but the addition of the news about Jesselene and the thought that she would be at church tempted her. She wouldn't have to pay attention to anything that was said.

Elder Harrison dived into a piece of Dutch chocolate cake with maple nut ice cream and didn't press her for a more definite answer. Megan had dozed off on her lap, so Elizabeth sat quietly watching the people around her. The friendliness and closeness between all these people drew her in, and she was content to sit back and bask in its warmth for a while. She could imagine Jesselene fitting right into this scene, pulling children to her lap and serving cake, all the while making each person feel as if he or she were the only one in the room.

Maybe she'd absolutely shock the socks off of Paul and go to church in the morning. Maybe she would. She turned to Elder Harrison. "Thank you for the invitation," she said. "I think we can probably be there tomorrow."

If Elder Harrison was surprised at her answer, he didn't show it. As he began explaining the different meetings and times, she tried to figure herself out. All she knew was that these Mormons had the ability to draw others to them, and she hadn't decided yet how they did it. But she did know she would enjoy meeting Jesselene tomorrow and feeling the special way Jesselene made her feel.

Paul could enjoy the religion part.

CHAPTER

13

"*Are you sure you want to do this?*" Paul asked, giving his tie one last tug.

Elizabeth was at her vanity, putting the finishing touches of make-up on her face. His question echoed the first thought she'd had upon waking that morning. She had decided then that she still wanted to do it, maybe not for the same reason he did, but what difference did that make? "Sure." Then she qualified the answer. "Just remember — this doesn't mean I want to become a Mormon. I just don't feel like staying home by myself today."

Handsome in his dark suit, he stood behind her, hands on her shoulders, and looked at her in the mirror. "You look pretty," he said.

"Thanks." She powdered her nose one more time and smiled up at him. Slipping away from his arms before he could hug her, she picked up her purse and took his hand. "Let's go get the baby before her dress gets wrinkled." She felt good to be leaving with Paul and Megan on a Sunday morning instead of sitting at the window in her bathrobe as Paul left for mass. He always looked so lonesome leaving by himself, and she always felt so left out on those mornings.

Several minutes later, though, her confidence faltered as they faced the doors of the church and saw the smiling faces of Elder Thorne and Elder Harrison, who enthusiastically opened the doors for them. Paul was behind Elizabeth, so he gave her a little nudge on her waist. Before she could think of a disease to have suddenly caught, she was inside.

The music had started, so the missionaries ushered them into the chapel. It was much plainer than any other church Elizabeth could remember from the times her different foster parents had insisted on her presence at a church. She followed meekly as a lamb until they got about four rows from the back. "Let's sit here," she whispered to Paul, pointing to an empty pew. "I don't want to be too far from the door in case I need to go out with Megan."

"Fine, sweetheart." He called to the elders already two pews ahead. "Let's sit here, guys."

"You bet," they both said.

Elder Harrison slipped in before Elizabeth and Megan. "I want to sit by the baby. I used to entertain my baby sister during church," he whispered.

"You have a baby sister?" she asked. "How many brothers and sisters do you have?"

"Ten," he said.

Elizabeth got light-headed at the thought. A man stood up at the podium and began the meeting, but Elder Harrison's answer had so distracted Elizabeth that she spent the first hymn and even the prayer counting all the children she could see and dividing them by the number of families. As nearly as she could figure without a calculator, the average came out to three and a half, which calmed her a little.

Between entertaining Megan and watching the little

family circuses going on all around her as mothers and fathers tried to keep their three-and-a-half children quiet, Elizabeth had plenty to do without worrying she might hear something she didn't want to hear. It wasn't until the first speaker was concluding that she spotted Jesselene. She was sitting way up front to the left. Elizabeth deduced from the back of the heads around Jesselene that she was sitting between her husband and her daughter. Jesselene was right—her daughter and Elizabeth did have the same color hair.

Totally out of character, Megan fell asleep on Elder Harrison's shoulder, trapping Elizabeth for the rest of the meeting. Then, as hard as she tried, she couldn't block the last speaker out. For one thing he spoke well and loudly. She found herself irresistibly drawn to his speech, which was basically the story of how his whole family came to be Mormons. The most interesting part came at the end when he stated what he knew to be true. She knew there was a distinct difference between actually knowing and only believing something, and this man kept saying that he knew the Mormon church was true, the Book of Mormon was true, and even a prophet whose name she couldn't remember was true. The man speaking sounded like a rational adult, and he did say he was a school principal, so he had to have a certain amount of intelligence. So how did he know that all these things were true?

Paul had leaned forward, elbows on knees, listening intently throughout the whole talk, so maybe he understood it. Suddenly the talk ended, and everyone began flipping through their hymnbooks. Elizabeth still felt his words echoing in the room. It was a strange feeling—like watching Paul in the courtroom and not believing that the man who spoke so eloquently to a jury was the same man who threw his dirty socks down on the bathroom floor.

She shook the echoes out of her head. Since Elder Harrison had stuck the hymnbook in front of her nose, she joined in singing quietly. Then someone said a prayer, and everyone began standing and shaking hands. Paul and the missionaries started to talk to the family in front of them, but Elizabeth stood up, waking Megan in the process, and slipped over to the other aisle so she could catch Jesselene as her family left.

She watched Jesselene, followed by a husband, a daughter, and a son, stop at almost every pew to pat a child on the head, hug a woman, and always bring a smile to whomever she spoke with. It was obvious to Elizabeth that she wasn't the only one drawn to Jesselene's kindness and attentions.

When Jesselene reached Elizabeth's pew, she stopped immediately, taken aback only for a minute, then gathered Elizabeth in a hug. "Elizabeth," she said, "how wonderful to see you here." She let Elizabeth go and pulled her husband away from the man he was talking to. "Rowland, dear, this is Elizabeth Danforth, the realtor I've told you about. And this is her precious little girl, Megan."

Rowland's hand warmly and firmly engulfed her hand. "I'm so pleased to meet you."

"Diane, Steve," she called, pulling them over to her. "This is Elizabeth Danforth. Elizabeth, my daughter, Diane, and my son, Steve."

"Hi," they both said. Then Diane reached for Megan, who snuggled farther into Elizabeth's shoulder. "What an adorable baby! Look at those big brown eyes."

Paul and the missionaries came up behind Elizabeth. "This is my husband, Paul," Elizabeth said. "And I guess you know the missionaries."

Introductions complete, Jesselene turned to Elizabeth inquiringly. "So you two are taking the discussions?"

"Well." Elizabeth hesitated, wondering if Jesselene would remember the boat conversation. Paul, not knowing anything about boat conversations, put his hands on Elizabeth's shoulders and explained. "I am. Elizabeth was good enough to come with me today."

"Oh," Jesselene said.

Elizabeth smiled weakly as Jesselene looked at her. In a split second, Elizabeth knew that Jesselene had figured her and their conversation out. Now she would probably think that Elizabeth was terrible and never want her to work at TLC again.

The look on Jesselene's face passed as quickly as it had come and was replaced by excitement. "Do you have any plans for dinner?" she asked.

Elizabeth looked up at Paul. "We were just going to eat out," he said.

"Oh no, please," Jesselene said. "We'd love for you to have dinner with us. I've got a huge lasagna waiting at home."

"Oh, we couldn't," Elizabeth protested.

"Yes, you can," Jesselene insisted. "Tell them, Rowland."

"We really would love to have you," Rowland said. "You elders too."

"Thanks, but we already have a dinner appointment," Elder Thorne said.

"See, that settles it," Jesselene said. "You're coming."

Elizabeth didn't see what that settled, but she decided to accept the invitation because she honestly couldn't think of anything she would like to do more.

Paul started to say something, but Elizabeth poked him in the side with her elbow. With an "umph," he hushed.

"We'd love to come," Elizabeth said. "It's wonderful of you to ask us."

Just then the Robertsons with their brood came up, happy to see them, and conversation flowed easily until the chapel emptied and they were the only ones still standing there.

"Well, maybe we'd better go," Jesselene said. "Nephi, Jeanine, would you like to join us for dinner too?"

"Thanks, anyway," Jeanine said. "But I left dinner in the oven." She looked at Nephi. "And if we don't get home soon, it just might be burned."

Surprised and excited, Elizabeth followed the Mannings out of the building—surprised that the morning had actually been pleasurable and excited that Jesselene seemed to want her over for dinner as much as she wanted to be there. Looking back, she smiled at Paul and winked, letting him know that the morning they had worried over had been fine. He winked in return. Reaching for her hand, he walked by her side out of church.

● ● ●

Jesselene's lasagna was as delicious as her family had promised it to be, and Paul loved her sourdough bread so much that Elizabeth was embarrassed by the amount he ate.

Elizabeth stood up to help clear the table, slapping Paul's hand as he reached for another piece of bread. "You have to give me the recipe for this bread," Elizabeth said.

"Yes, please do," Paul begged.

"Well, maybe not," Elizabeth said. "You'd be too fat to fit through the courtroom door." She snatched away the plate with the rest of the bread on it and laid it on the kitchen counter, where Jesselene promptly picked the plate up and put it back in front of Paul.

"Are you a judge?" Steve asked Paul.

"No," he mumbled through a mouthful of bread. "A lawyer."

"A lawyer?" Steve said, clearly awestruck. "Gosh! Have you ever defended a murderer?"

"Steve!" Jesselene said.

Paul laughed as he finally pushed himself away from the

table. "Come on, and I'll tell you about all the infamous criminals I've ever known." With his arm around Steve's shoulders, they went into the den. Rowland had already sunk into his recliner with the newspaper, and Diane was browsing through photo albums with Megan.

In the kitchen, Elizabeth said, "I really would like to know how to make this bread. I'm not much of a cook."

"Didn't your mother cook much?" Jesselene asked.

"No."

They busied themselves with scraping plates and loading the dishwasher. Jesselene was as efficient in the kitchen as she was at TLC. Elizabeth usually dragged her way through the dishes, but with Jesselene the dishwasher was full in no time. Jesselene put the last dish in, shut the door, and wiped her hands on her apron before turning to Elizabeth. "So, do your parents live around here?"

"No," Elizabeth said. "Both of my parents died when I was young." That was what she always said, speaking of the people who would have been her adoptive parents had they lived. It had always seemed easier to explain things that way.

"Oh, I'm sorry," Jesselene said. "So who raised you?"

Elizabeth knew that Jesselene would have listened sympathetically, maybe even offering some insight to help her accept her past, but Elizabeth just didn't want anything to spoil the pleasant afternoon in the Manning home. She was saved from making an excuse about her past by Diane coming back into the kitchen, Megan in one arm, a photo album under the other.

Megan jumped into Elizabeth's arms, and Diane laid the photo album on the table and opened it. "See, Mom." She pointed to some pictures of a baby about Megan's age. "I told you Megan looks like I did when I was a baby."

Elizabeth and Jesselene both looked where she was pointing. Some of the pictures could have come out of

Megan's album. "You're right, hon'," Jesselene said. She smoothed down Megan's hair against Elizabeth's shoulder, where she lay sucking her thumb drowsily. "Hopefully, she'll grow up to be just as pretty as her mommy."

"Maybe we should look at our genealogy to see if we're related somehow," Diane suggested.

"What's a genealogy?" Elizabeth asked.

Jesselene and Diane exchanged a glance not understood by Elizabeth. Jesselene tucked her arm into Elizabeth's, drawing her into the den where the men were deep in conversation. "Oh, there's plenty of time for talk about genealogy," Jesselene said. "Let's bore you to death with these albums Diane pulls out every Sunday afternoon."

"I'd love to see them—really," Elizabeth said. And, of course, she meant it.

The next couple of hours passed easily, interrupted by a wonderful chocolate cake, while Megan dozed on a blanket on the floor. Dusk was settling when Rowland got up from his recliner and walked over to the bookcase to take out a large softcover book. Steve sat up a little straighter on the couch, and Diane adjusted the pillows behind her back on the floor as if to settle in more comfortably for something.

Rowland eased back into his chair and flipped open the book, smoothing the page down. "Paul, Elizabeth," he said, "we usually have a short lesson on Sunday evenings and study our scriptures. Would that be all right with you?"

"That would be fine with me," Paul spoke up. He was seated on the floor by Elizabeth, who was sitting on the couch. "How about you, Bets?"

"Sure," she said. What else could she say? No, I won't stand for it, and I'm going to leave right now? She was enjoying her afternoon so much she didn't want to leave, and she certainly didn't want Jesselene to think she was some kind of strange person who hated God. So, once again, she willed herself to become a spectator instead of a participant.

This time she wasn't very successful, though. She tried to focus on the family pictures on the wall, the two cracked keys on the piano next to her, even the dust around the lamp on the bookcase, but it didn't work. Her attention kept going back to the family before her, sitting close and warm together, laughing and reading, drawing her husband and even her into their circle of love. It was just the kind of family scene she'd always pictured for herself as a child. She envied Diane and Steve their childhood, their home, and their parents, wishing she could have fit into such a family too.

She hadn't even said a word, but when their lesson and prayer were over, she was disappointed. What was it about these Mormons? They all made her feel emotions she had never experienced before.

After another half hour or so, Paul and Elizabeth left, though Jesselene begged them to stay for an evening snack. Elizabeth was loathe to go, but she felt that staying any longer, or letting Paul eat any more, would be an imposition. Jesselene said that was silly, and to prove it, she sent Paul home with a bag of rolls and another piece of cake and pressed Elizabeth to come by any morning that week and see her at TLC.

The ride home was pretty quiet — until they were almost home. It had taken Elizabeth that long to work up the nerve to ask Paul what she wanted. "Paul?"

"Yeah?" He yawned sleepily.

"Now that you're a hotshot lawyer" — she hoped she had loosened him up with that comment — "I want you to help me look for my mother again."

"Bets," he moaned. "We've tried before and had no success."

"I know, but then you weren't a partner in a law firm.

Surely someone has some connections that could help me, or knows someone who does." They were in their driveway now, and she turned to face him. He was staring out his window, tapping the car keys against the steering wheel. "Isn't that a possibility?"

He turned to face her. "I guess so. But why, Bets, why all of a sudden have you decided to do this again? Can't you just be happy with Megan and me? Don't you think there are other people in the world who would like to rewrite their childhood? But you can't do that."

There was an edge of sorrow to her voice. "I am happy with you and Megan. I love you both. But there's always a part of me that feels as if I don't belong anywhere because I don't belong to anyone in my past."

"Did something happen this afternoon to make you start thinking of this again?"

"No," she said defensively. "Well, maybe, yes. A family happened. I envy the Mannings their family. They have something that I've never had."

"You still wouldn't have a childhood like that even if you found your mother."

"I know, but maybe I'll understand why I didn't have it." She was determined not to give up this time. "Besides, you owe it to me."

"Why?" he asked, eyes narrowing.

"Haven't I been understanding of you asking all these questions about the Mormon church? And," she pressed further, "didn't I spend the morning with you at church?"

"So now I owe you?"

"No." She smiled. "I'm just reminding you how wonderful I've been the last couple of days."

He didn't answer for a minute. When he finally did, he put his arm on the seat behind her. "That's my point. You are wonderful, and I love you. I don't want you to be hurt again. I honestly think there's very little chance that we'll find anything out about your mother since we couldn't the last time."

Elizabeth was not going to be deterred. "I promise you I won't be hurt if you'll just try. Just think about it. Can't you promise me that?"

He considered that. "I'll think about it. But that's all I promise." He got out of the car before she could plead further.

It was more than she thought he would give her. She had been sure he would turn her down flat. As she unbuckled Megan, she felt excited and wished she had a friend she could share this slight ray of hope with. Maybe she would take Jesselene up on her offer to visit her this week and tell her all about it. Hadn't she said she'd like to hear Elizabeth's long story sometime? With her wonderful family, Jesselene couldn't understand the emptiness Elizabeth felt not know-ing who her family was. But as kind as Jesselene was, Eliz-abeth knew she would try her best to understand.

CHAPTER

14

For some reason, Jesselene slept fitfully, waking, then drifting off to an uneasy sleep, only to wake again. Very early in the morning, as she lay still so as not to disturb Rowland, she decided she might as well get up. She slipped out of bed, pulled her robe about her, and walked through the darkness of the house to the den, where only hours before it had been filled with family and friendship. Since they hadn't lit a fire, the room was chilly. She pulled an afghan around her as she sat in the dark.

She thought about Paul and Elizabeth. She was sure that the problem Elizabeth had hinted at the other day was Paul's interest in the Church and her disinterest. Through-out the years, she and Rowland had brought enough people into the Church to recognize the spark in Paul's eyes. He was so ready. But Elizabeth was another matter. She had seemed so distant when they were having their family home evening lesson that Jesselene wondered if perhaps they should have just skipped it while the Danforths were there. Elizabeth hadn't asked a single question or made even the tiniest comment the whole time.

While she pondered that, another thought surfaced as it had several times during the afternoon. She'd kept pushing it away, but now that she was alone in the room, it seemed okay to think it. She was used to being drawn to young women who were about the age of what her baby girl would now be, but it had never occurred to her to go one generation further and consider the possibility that her daughter would have her own children—that she would be a grandmother. But, seeing Elizabeth with Megan had made her think of that, and suddenly she felt cheated of not only a daughter, but perhaps even grandchildren.

"Jesselene?" Rowland came up quietly behind her.

"Rowland, honey?" she said. "You startled me."

"Are you all right?" He sat down beside her.

She patted his knee. "I'm fine. I'm just thinking."

His brows knit together with concern. "About what?"

"Nothing really. Just about Paul and Elizabeth. Don't you think they'd make good members of the Church?"

"Great ones," he said. "Paul and I had a chance to talk, and he is really serious about the Church. Elizabeth isn't at all interested, though, he said."

"Why not?"

"He didn't, or wouldn't, say. He said it was a long story."

"Funny," Jesselene said. "That's the same thing she said to me. I wonder . . . "

"Don't start wondering," he said. "You'll never get to sleep."

"Well, I think I'll make sure to see her a couple of times this week. Maybe I can get her more interested."

"That's just what you need—another cause to work on."

Her thoughts turned into words and slipped out before she even thought about it. "I can't help it," she said. "My daughter would be about that age."

"So that's it," he said. "That's why you're up."

She knew she shouldn't have said what she said. Rowland sounded so sad, for her or for himself having to go through this again. She wasn't sure which.

"Elizabeth can't take the place of your daughter, Jesselene. She needs a friend, not a mother."

Jesselene didn't tell him what Elizabeth had said about her parents being killed. It would be better just to drop the whole thing. She knew from experience that this feeling of loss would fade. Then she'd push it back into a little corner of her life, where it would wait until something else reminded her of her lost daughter. "I know, I know, hon'," she said. "Now don't go and give me a lecture. I'm fine, and I'm certainly not going to go out and file adoption papers on Elizabeth today."

They walked slowly back to the bedroom, arms around each other, and both deep in their own thoughts. As they reached the door and Rowland stepped aside to let Jesselene go first, Jesselene thought pensively that only she knew that a part of her had gone with her baby that day.

● ● ●

That morning, Paul could feel Bets's wordless question about looking for her mother and sensed that she wanted an answer before he left. But she didn't ask him.

As he looked at her, though, he knew that he would do everything he possibly could to help her find her mother. How could he deny her that when she brought him so much happiness? He really didn't believe that it was possible to find her mother, but maybe if he did all he could, she could put the matter to rest. Then at last the pain that came so quickly to her eyes when she thought of her past would finally dwindle to nothing. So he would do it—a few ideas had occurred to him since last night—but he wasn't going to let her know until he checked them out.

He could still feel her unspoken question as he left, but

he pretended he didn't notice. Giving her one more hug, he disentangled himself from her arms to pick up his brief-case. "Love you," he said. "See you tonight." Then he walked out the door.

"'Bye," she called out. Grabbing the door before it closed, she watched him walk out to the car.

Again he resisted the temptation to turn around and say, "Yes, I'm going to do it. So cross your fingers and maybe we'll get lucky."

• • •

"So, if that's all the business we need to discuss, we're finished," Ben said. He looked around at the men sitting at the polished table. Most of them had begun closing their notebooks and snapping shut their briefcases. Only Paul was sitting still, chewing on the eraser of a pencil. "Paul, you have anything?"

Paul hesitated a moment, then took the pencil from his mouth and began tapping it on the table. "Yes," he said, "I need to know if anyone knows a judge or lawyer up in the Pittsburgh area—someone who could help me with an adoption search."

The boss looked puzzled. "We don't usually handle those cases, do we?"

"Actually, it's a family matter," Paul explained. "Is that a problem?"

"Of course not," Ben said. "Can anyone help Paul?" he asked, looking around the table.

Dan waved his hand. "I've got a brother-in-law who practices there. I could give you his number, and you could see what he can do."

"Thanks." Paul brightened. So far it was simple.

"Let me give my wife a call and get the number. I'll bring it to you when I get it."

"Thanks," Paul said again. Now he began gathering up his papers, his mind racing. Maybe Bets was right. Maybe he could find her mother, and Bets would be happier than he ever thought she could be . . . He looked up to see Nephi standing before him.

"How was your dinner at the Mannings?" Nephi asked.

"Great," Paul said. "Bets especially enjoyed it."

"Good," Nephi said. Then, "Can I ask you something?"

"Shoot."

"Is this adoption search about Bets?"

"How did you figure that out?" Paul wondered if anyone else had guessed. Would Bets mind him telling Nephi about it? He couldn't decide, but he expected Nephi to be full of questions, as any experienced lawyer would be.

He wasn't, however. Instead, all he said was "If there's anything I can do to help, just let me know."

"I appreciate that." Then, just because Nephi hadn't asked, Paul wanted him to know. Leaning back in the chair, briefcase balancing on his knees, he prepared to tell Nephi what he had never mentioned to anyone else. "I wish I could find who Bets's mother is. It has haunted her all her life that she doesn't have any family and doesn't know who she belongs to."

"Doesn't she have her adoptive family?"

"That's the main problem, Nephi," Paul said. "The couple who adopted her died in a car accident a few months after the adoption. From then on, she was just sort of shuffled from one foster home to another and never really belonged to any of them."

"I can see where that could affect her even now," Nephi said.

"That's why she's not interested in the Church," Paul said, not believing he was saying it. "In a way, I guess she blames God for not giving her a family, and she's refused to have anything to do with any religion for as long as I've known her."

A light flashed on in Nephi's eyes, and Paul knew that he understood now why Bets was so reluctant to have any contact with the Church. Nephi had seemed so inspired about other questions that Paul thought maybe he'd have some new insight on this problem.

"Now I see," Nephi said. But that was all he said. He offered nothing inspired, nothing new. And he had no time to come up with anything because Nephi's secretary poked her head into the door and told him he had a long-distance call waiting. He put his hand on Paul's shoulder and looked at him compassionately. "It will all work out, Paul, I'm sure. We'll have faith, and we'll be there for her. Just let me know what Jeanine and I can do."

He left, and Paul sat alone with his thoughts for a while, trying to have faith, even though he still wasn't sure what that meant. He hoped that this search wouldn't leave Bets heartbroken again.

Not until the afternoon was he able to get in touch with the brother-in-law, who was very willing to help — for a fee Paul was sure, although nothing was mentioned. As he hung up the phone after talking to him, he sat staring at the receiver, wondering if he should call Bets. He flipped open a folder, sighed, snapped the folder shut, picked up the phone again, and dialed. "Bets?" he said.

"Hey," she said, surprised. He didn't call her very often in the middle of an afternoon. "Anything wrong?"

"No," he said slowly. He knew that, as soon as he told her what he'd done, she would be on cloud nine. "Nothing's wrong. Now, don't get your hopes all up, but Dan gave me the name of a brother-in-law he has in Pennsylvania who handles adoption cases. I just talked to him, and he's going to check out a few things about your adoption."

"Oh Paul!" she squealed. "You did it! You decided to

help me. What did you say to him? What did he say? Tell me everything."

"I think I have. It wasn't much. About all I had to give him was your name, the name of the couple who adopted you, and the initials inside your ring."

"I just know we're going to get lucky this time."

"Maybe so," he said. His voice was not encouraging. "Maybe so."

"Oh, don't be so negative," she teased.

"Just don't get your hopes up. Promise?"

"Cross my heart," she said.

His other line was blinking. "I've got to go, sweetheart."

"'Bye," she said. "And, honey?"

"What?"

"Thanks. I love you."

"Love you too," he said. And that is exactly why I've gotten myself in something I don't want to be involved in.

● ● ●

Elizabeth didn't say much to Paul that night after he came home because she knew he'd keep cautioning her not to get her hopes too high. She felt like a child at Christmas wanting a gift so badly it hurt to think about the possibility that she might not get it. Goodness knows, that had happened to her several times as a child. So, while she calmly folded the clothes she'd washed that day, she asked only one time for a verbatim repeat of the telephone conversation, then remarked serenely, "It will be interesting to see what he comes up with."

A little later, as Elizabeth was putting stacks of folded clothes into the basket, the phone rang. "I'll get that," Paul said. She had started to go up the stairs with the basket, not paying any attention to Paul's phone conversation, when he put his hand over the receiver and called her.

"Bets, it's Elder Thorne. They want to come over tomorrow night and teach me the second lesson. I was thinking that maybe we could have them over for dinner too."

"Dinner? Over here?" Paul was crazy.

"What do you think?" he asked. He gestured to the phone, indicating that Elder Thorne was waiting for an answer.

"I don't know," she said. "I don't know what I would fix. And Carla's invited all the wives for lunch. I really think she wants to check out Jeanine once more."

"Oh, well, I guess they can come over just for the lesson. Maybe we can invite them for dinner at another time."

But, as Elizabeth gazed fondly at her husband who had done so much for her, she found herself saying, "Actually, I guess I'll still have enough time to fix a simple dinner for everyone. The lunch won't take all day. Okay, let's invite them. But remember—"

"I know, you don't want to have anything to do with the discussion." He blew her a kiss and went back to the phone. "Thanks."

As he finished talking with the missionaries, Elizabeth picked up a pad and pencil from the table beside her. "Now, let's make a list of everything I fix well."

"That shouldn't take long," Paul said, hanging up the phone. He had barely finished his sentence before the pillow she threw hit him in the head.

15

"Wait, wait," Jeanine said. *She tugged on* Elizabeth's arm and pulled her back behind the lattice divider between the foyer and dining floor of the restaurant. "Let's find the restroom before we go in so I can see how I look." Jeanine had been primping since she had climbed into Elizabeth's car. She was really nervous about lunch with all the wives.

"Why don't we find the restroom and climb out the window and escape?" Elizabeth asked. She really wanted to spend some time that morning at TLC and wasn't looking forward to the luncheon at all.

Jeanine giggled. "She hasn't seen us yet. We could save ruining our hose and just walk back through the door."

"Let's go."

"We couldn't," Jeanine said. "Could we? We ought to go for our husbands' sake."

"I don't know. I wonder what Paul would think. What do you think Nephi would say?"

"He told me this morning I should just call and say I couldn't come because I was such a nervous wreck."

"Carla really is harmless," Elizabeth said. "She's more

irritating than anything, I guess. She's just never forgiven me for deciding not to go back to work after Megan was born."

"She'll love me then," Jeanine said.

The hostess approached them, oversized menus in hand. From the look on her face, she seemed to be wondering if the two nicely dressed women hiding behind the spider plants had spent too much time at the lounge across the street. "Hi, I'm Marie, the hostess," she said. "May I seat you?"

"Yes," Jeanine said.

"No," Elizabeth said. Then they both giggled.

"Pardon me?" Marie the hostess said.

"Elizabeth, we can't," Jeanine said.

"I bet we can." Elizabeth moved the spider plant over and pointed through the lattice work. "See that woman in the hat sitting at the table with those four other women?" she asked the hostess.

First glancing around to see if anyone was watching her, Marie the hostess inched forward and peeked around the spider plant. "The purple hat? The one on her second whiskey sour?"

"That's her," Elizabeth said. "Can you give her a message for me?"

"Sure."

"Tell her that Elizabeth and Jeanine say they're sorry, but something came up, and they won't be able to stay for lunch."

Marie the hostess was writing it on the back of a menu. "That's all?" she asked.

"That's it," Elizabeth said. She pulled a five-dollar bill out of her wallet and stuffed it in Marie's hand. "And," she added dramatically, "if anyone, I mean anyone, asks, don't tell them anything."

"I won't," the hostess said. "I promise."

She scurried off to deliver her important message as Elizabeth and Jeanine pushed their way back through the door into the sunlight where they collapsed giggling against the wall. "You're awful," Jeanine said. "I've never played hookey before."

"I have," Elizabeth said. "But never from spinach quiche."

"Oh," Jeanine said, "I love spinach quiche."

"Want to go back in and get some?"

"No," Jeanine said emphatically. They started walking slowly back to the car. "But what should we do now? I hate to waste a babysitter."

Reaching the BMW, they got inside and sat with the motor running. Neither of them wanted to go shopping, and Jeanine didn't have enough time for a matinee, so Elizabeth finally suggested what she had wanted to do all morning. "We could go by TLC and see if there's anything we could do to help Jesselene."

"That's a great idea," Jeanine said. "Are you sure she's there?"

"She told me Sunday she'd be there every day this week."

"Then let's go."

Elizabeth backed the car out and wove her way through the traffic toward TLC. Jeanine remarked that she had not been through that particular part of town yet, so Elizabeth pointed out some points of interest along the way. Jeanine didn't say much in response, but when they pulled up in front of TLC, she suddenly asked, "So what did you think about church Sunday, Elizabeth?"

Elizabeth hesitated, wondering how she had felt about it, but couldn't come up with anything concrete. What stood out most instead was the afternoon with the Mannings. "Well . . . " She smiled at Jeanine. "It wasn't as bad as I thought it would be."

"Hmmm," Jeanine said, smiling back. "I guess that's good."

"Is it?"

"I'm not sure, but I think it is." She smiled slyly. "Maybe you'll like it better next time."

"Oh" was all Elizabeth said as they got out of the car.

Jesselene was happy to see them when they located her in the back room, unloading several boxes of baby clothes. "Isn't this wonderful?" she said, sweeping her arm over the boxes. "A church had a yard sale and donated all the baby clothes they didn't sell. There must be fifty little stretch suits here."

Her enthusiasm was contagious. "We'll help you unpack them," Elizabeth said.

"Thanks, hon'," Jesselene said. Then she noticed how they were dressed. "But you two are dressed too nicely to get down on the floor and unpack boxes. You look like you've been out to lunch in a fancy restaurant."

"Well, almost," Elizabeth said. She looked at Jeanine, and they both burst out giggling again.

Jesselene looked puzzled. "What have you two been up to?"

So they told her, and she giggled with them. "Shame on you," she said. "You need to do something good to repent." She pushed a box toward them.

Jeanine already looked penitent. "I guess it wasn't very nice. I feel sort of bad about it." She looked over at Elizabeth seriously, and Elizabeth was afraid she was going to demand they publicly apologize to Carla. "And you know what the worst part is?"

"No," Elizabeth asked, not really wanting to hear.

"I'm starving," Jeanine said. They all collapsed in giggles again.

Elizabeth hadn't had such a good time since, well, since yesterday at the Mannings' home. What was it about these

Mormons? They reminded her of Velcro. You got close to them and they sort of stuck to you. The more afraid she became of their beliefs and religion, the more drawn she was to the Mormon people she knew.

Not speaking much, except to hold up an especially cute outfit, they each worked folding little stretch suits and putting them on the proper shelves. Within fifteen minutes, they were finished and stood back to gaze at the full shelves.

"Doesn't that look better?" Jesselene asked. "It will be so nice to actually give the women a choice of clothes."

"Have you seen any women yet this morning?" Jeanine asked.

"A couple," Jesselene said. "They both needed formula and juice."

"I think what you're doing is wonderful," Jeanine said. "Was this your idea?"

"I guess so," Jesselene said. "I knew it was something that Waynesboro needed, and I just hoped and prayed that the community would support it." She smiled first at Jeanine, then at Elizabeth. "So far they have."

"I know you're going to help a lot of babies and their mothers," Jeanine said. "I'm glad that I can be a part of it."

Elizabeth laid her hand on a pile of soft clothes and let their conversation wander in and out of her mind. Would her mother have come to a place like this and found the support she needed to keep her baby? Where were the people who loved her mother when she — and Elizabeth — had needed them? But there were no more answers in that little storage room than there had been anyplace else throughout her life.

She felt a hand on her arm. "Are you all right?" Jesselene asked. "You look so sad again."

Elizabeth turned back to them as the desire to empty her heart to these two new but dear friends swept over her.

Only a single naked lightbulb burned over them, but Elizabeth felt warmth in the room that seemed to flow around the three of them, drawing them together. Her old hurts welled up in her throat, wanting to become words. Jesselene and Jeanine waited, knowing she wanted to say something. Could they see and feel the light, too? She opened her mouth to speak, not even knowing how she would begin.

The bell over the front office door jangled, signaling need. "Is anybody here?" a voice called.

Jesselene hesitated a few seconds, searching Elizabeth's face for a clue to what she had been about to say.

"I'm fine," Elizabeth said. "Not sad at all." She smiled. "Just hungry."

"Okay," Jesselene said. But Elizabeth didn't feel as if she really believed her. "I'll be right there," Jesselene called.

She left, leaving Elizabeth to look at Jeanine, who also looked puzzled. But Elizabeth ignored it, asking instead, "Want to order a pizza?"

"Sounds good to me," Jeanine said. "Of course, we could always catch dessert with Carla."

They giggled again as Elizabeth followed Jeanine out of the back room and, with a long regretful look back into the lighted room, reached over to turn off the light.

● ● ●

Several hours of cooking and Paul's help resulted in dinner being on the table at exactly six-thirty. A little earlier, while Elizabeth and Paul were both in the kitchen, Elizabeth filled him in on her day and how she and Jeanine had played hookey from lunch.

"We were terrible, weren't we?" she asked.

"It doesn't bother me," he said with a smile. "I don't think I'll get fired."

"It bothered Jeanine. I don't think she very often does things like that."

"Nephi might not let you play with her anymore," Paul teased.

Then Elder Harrison and Elder Thorne had pleased her by riding up on their bicycles promptly at six. Elder Thorne had entertained Megan, and Elder Harrison put the ice in the glasses which, if they were trying to impress her, they certainly did.

For some reason everything turned out delicious, which was not something Elizabeth was accustomed to with her cooking. All three men raved about her roast and rolls.

"Sweetheart," Paul said, "these rolls are delicious."

"They're really good," Elder Harrison said. He took what must have been his sixth one and buttered it.

"Have you two had anything to eat today?" Elizabeth asked Elder Thorne. "You seem so hungry."

"I'm sorry," he said. He pulled his hand back from reaching for the bowl of mashed potatoes. "I guess we didn't have much to eat today."

"No, please," Paul said. He spooned some more potatoes on Elder Thorne's plate. "Eat all you want."

They did. And soon dinner was over because all the food was gone. Elizabeth began clearing the table. She was happy because she could not remember many times that her cooking had been appreciated so much.

With the missionaries' help, the table was soon cleared. But as Elizabeth reached for the dessert plates, Paul steered her away from the counter. "Let's eat dessert after the discussion, Bets," he said. "Is that okay with you two?"

"You bet," they both said.

Elizabeth had planned on Megan being so sleepy that she would have no other choice but take her upstairs to bed, forcing Elizabeth to miss the lesson. But Megan seemed to be content as Elder Thorne carried her into the den behind Paul and Elizabeth and sat her down in her pile of toys. She attacked them with more energy than she had had all week.

Paul continued to steer Elizabeth all the way to the couch, where he ever so gently pushed her down. "We'll sit here," he said. "You two grab those two chairs."

After settling down, Elder Harrison nodded to Elder Thorne, who cleared his throat and began. "We would like to thank you for having us here in your home tonight, Brother and Sister Danforth. We would like to begin with a prayer. Brother Danforth, since this is your home, we would like you to call on someone to offer that prayer. But we would like you to offer that prayer if you would. Would you do that?"

A cold chill swept over Elizabeth. In all the years that Paul had been such a devout Catholic, Elizabeth had never heard him pray out loud. She was sure he would be embarrassed. She felt so sorry for her husband. Putting her hand on his knees in unspoken support, she looked up at him as he said, "I'd be glad to pray."

Her mouth dropped open, her whole body sagged, and she stared at the man beside her who bowed his head, clasped his hands between his knees, and began to pray. It was short and mentioned something about knowing what was right, and by the time it was over, Elizabeth was still staring. She shook her head in astonishment just as they all opened their eyes.

Although he didn't look at her, Paul shifted on the couch to put his arm behind her. The phone refused to ring, Megan refused to cry, and the smoke alarm remained quiet. She was definitely stuck on the couch.

The missionaries began to talk about things that she had never spent a millisecond thinking about. Trying not to pay attention became more difficult as Paul answered their questions with such thoughtfulness and sincerity that

Elizabeth became convinced that he had spent a lot of time studying and reading.

Strangely, though, it didn't scare her, and as she began to relax, she thought that the light in the room seemed brighter, even though no one else seemed to notice, and a warm feeling began to surround her. Although she tried not to be, she was drawn into their discussion. They began to speak about repentance and the peace that comes through receiving forgiveness for your sins. She didn't know exactly what she needed to be forgiven for, but when they spoke of peace, her heart seemed to burn within her, and she knew that peace must be the elusive feeling she had struggled all her life to have. But even as she couldn't deny the feelings she was having, she couldn't understand how these two young men could have what she had searched for over so many years.

She contemplated that as Elder Harrison began to read from the Book of Mormon. Paul was following along in his book, so she shifted her eyes, trying to find where they were without them knowing she was looking. But she didn't need to read. The words were simple ones that she heard every day of her life, but when they were put together in the sentences from the Book of Mormon, they seemed to come alive and leap out at her to burn themselves into her heart.

It took her breath away in an experience that she had never come close to having before. But still it didn't scare her, and gradually the intensity faded to a comfortable, almost familiar feeling. When the missionaries closed their book, Elizabeth knew that the lesson was over. She bit her lip not to ask the question that was on her tongue. Paul leaned forward as if to catch every last word Elder Thorne was saying.

"Brother Danforth," he said, "we've talked tonight about baptism and its importance in obeying Heavenly Father's commandments. We would like to ask you tonight if you would make a commitment to obey the commandment of baptism. If you will do that, we can pick out a day, and it will give you something to work toward." They both stared at Paul. "Do you think you could do that?"

Sighing deeply, Paul leaned back without responding. The missionaries waited silently while Paul glanced down at Elizabeth with a look somewhere between apology and determination. At that moment, Elizabeth realized that he was not hesitating because of indecision or doubt but because he was afraid of how she felt. She considered saying, "Paul, do what you have to" or "Paul, if you do, I'll leave you," but she couldn't decide which one she wanted, so she waited with bated breath.

"I'd like to be baptized," he said.

The missionaries broke into smiles and, it seemed to her, carefully avoided her eyes. Elizabeth decided it was time to put Megan to bed. "I'll get her to bed," she said, picking her up. "You can cut everyone a piece of cake if you'd like, Paul."

"Sure, sweetheart."

She left the room and didn't catch who said the prayer. Upstairs, as she put Megan in her pajamas and settled her down with blanket and pacifier, she tried to feel betrayed, but she couldn't. About all she could muster was indifference, until she walked into the kitchen. Then what she was surprised to feel was a slight envy at the three men around the table. Two were so young and enthusiastic, and yet they had some ability or maybe power to convince her husband, so accustomed to resisting the persuasive arguments of experienced lawyers, to make a total change in their lives. And this ability, or power, had touched her also. She envied them all the conviction they had.

Talk flowed around school and family as they ate their cake, and nothing more was mentioned about the baptism or the Church before the missionaries left. Paul saw them to the door while Elizabeth finished up in the kitchen. As she washed the last pan, he came quietly up behind her and put his arms around her.

"I guess you're mad at me," he said.

"No, I'm not," she answered, not turning around.

"You're not?"

"I guess I saw it coming." She shook the water off the pan and placed it in the dish drainer before turning to face him. "I just wish it were so important to me."

"Maybe it will be," he said. He caught her hands and squeezed them. "It's good and it's true, Bets, and I don't see how it could do anything but make me love you and Megan more than I already do—if that's possible."

"I hope so, honey," she said. "I hope so." It was her turn to bury her face in his shoulder. There they stood with him gently rocking her, not saying a word, until the baby's cry broke into their thoughts.

"I thought she was asleep," Elizabeth said.

"I'll go," Paul said.

"No, I will." She pulled herself away from him reluctantly and didn't look at him directly until she paused at the door. "Tell me something, Paul, if you can."

He leaned back against the sink to drink a glass of water. "Okay."

"What do we have to repent of to have peace? I mean, we haven't killed anybody or anything."

He didn't act too surprised as he answered. "No, but I guess everyone has things wrong in their lives—unkindness, bad temper, dishonesty. Nobody's perfect. I'm sure you could come up with a couple of minor things I'm guilty of." He smiled. "Nothing major, I hope."

She smiled back, but "Oh" was all she said as he looked at her seriously. She examined her life for those faults as she walked up the stairs. But when she reached the top, a tiny voice came from somewhere and echoed the words into her mind. Maybe, it said, maybe blaming God for your problems is the biggest fault of all.

16

Paul sat in his office the next day, files and notepads before him, but by ten o'clock he still had not accomplished a single constructive thing, so deep in thought was he about what Bets had asked him the night before. It had been a simple question—less than ten words—"What do we have to repent of?"—but it signaled such a drastic departure from anything she had ever said before that the thought of it totally distracted him from his work.

Why would she ask that if she hadn't paid at least some attention to what had been said last night? Had she felt the Spirit there, too, as strongly as he had? Did that one question mean there was even the slightest chance she would be interested in the gospel? The questions were driving him crazy. He should just pick up the phone and ask her.

He picked it up, as he already had several times that morning, but just as quickly put it down again. If she was becoming interested in the Church, then his saying anything about it might touch off that stubborn streak of hers. She might think that he was trying to pressure her. He would have to be patient.

He would be able to tell one thing, though, when he got home. Before he had gone to bed the night before, he had set a sort of trap to see if she had read the Book of Mormon while he was at work. She always insisted that magazines be stacked neatly with the largest ones on the bottom and *Reader's Digest* on top. He had deliberately stacked the magazines on his desk in the den in alphabetical order with *McCall's* on the bottom, topped by *People*, *Reader's Digest*, the larger *Time* magazine, then the Book of Mormon. He had left the Reader's Digest sticking out a little so that, if she picked up the Book of Mormon, she couldn't resist straightening them out according to size. It was a brilliant plan.

While he considered the previously unthought-of problem that she might notice the alphabetized magazines and straighten them out without reading the Book of Mormon, his secretary's voice instructed him to pick up line one to speak to Wayne Howard, the lawyer from Pennsylvania. Just what he didn't need was another problem in finding Bets's mother. "Hello, Wayne," Paul said. "I didn't expect to hear from you so soon."

"Well, it isn't real good news, I'm afraid," Wayne said.

"You didn't have any luck?

"Some, but not enough. We did get our hands on the adoption papers, listing the mother's name as Karen Lassiter, which goes with the initials on the ring."

Paul scribbled the name down, knowing as he did so that Bets would be thrilled with even this much. At last the faceless mother of her past had a name.

"We traced the mother to an address in a small town nearby, but that was the end of the trail. That particular street has since been turned over to condominiums. There were no Lassiters listed in any towns nearby."

"I appreciate this," Paul said. "Having a name is certainly much more than we've ever had before."

"I think that's about all we're going to be able to come up with unless you hire a private detective. The family evidently moved, and it would be very difficult to find them."

"I think so, too," Paul said.

"I'll send you all this information in a letter, of course," Wayne said.

"Thanks," Paul said. "Just let me know how much I owe you."

"I will," Wayne laughed.

So this was good news and bad news. Bets would be so happy to know her mother's name but so unhappy to hear how difficult it would be to find her. He hoped that he could convince her to be satisfied with the name and lay her fragmented past to rest. Sure, he laughed to himself. Then she would call the missionaries and beg to be baptized when he was, and they'd live happily ever.

● ● ●

Elizabeth had finished a hundred pages of the Book of Mormon when Paul called. She probably would not have even picked it up, but Paul had left a stack of magazines in an absolute mess on his desk. As she was straightening them up, she picked up the Book of Mormon, which was thrown on top. She had flipped through it, listing in her mind all the reasons she could think of not to sit down and read it. But Megan was taking an unusual morning nap, and she felt a strong curiosity pull her into the book.

So she had spent her morning reading the Book of Mormon, stopping often with her finger holding her place to close the book and stare at the cover, wondering how such a simple book with such funny names could be so real to her. It was at one of these moments of contemplation that Paul called.

"Hi, honey," she said. "What's up?" She put the book down quickly as if he could see her over the phone reading it.

"Well," he began. "I don't know if you're going to think that this is good news or bad news."

She caught her breath quickly, her chest tightening. "You heard from the lawyer?"

"Yes."

"So tell me."

"Well," he said. "Good news first. He was able to find her name."

"My mother's name? You know her name?" She grabbed at Paul's desk, searching for paper and pencil. At last she found some. "So what is it?"

"Let me tell you this first, sweetheart. He wasn't able to find her. The trail stopped cold because where she used to live was torn down for condominiums years ago. It was impossible to trace her from there."

"Oh." Disappointment clogged her throat and filled her eyes.

"I'm sorry, Bets. I know how you must feel." They said nothing for a minute.

"What's her name?" Elizabeth asked quietly.

"Karen Lassiter."

"Karen Lassiter." She repeated it as she wrote it down on the notepad although the name burned itself into her thoughts. "Is that all?" she asked.

"That's it, I think," Paul said. "He's going to be sending me a letter with everything in it he found out."

"Thank you, Paul. I know you didn't want to do this, but I appreciate it." She traced around her mother's name over and over.

"Are you okay?"

"I'll be fine."

"I'll try to be home early. I've got a terrible headache."

"Have you taken something for it?"

"Not yet, but I will."

"'Bye."

"'Bye, Bets. Call me if you need me."

Her mother's name. Karen. She had always liked the name Karen.

Without thinking, she marked her place in the Book of Mormon with the paper, then took it out and carefully placed the Book of Mormon on the neatly stacked magazines. Why was Paul so sloppy about stacking books and magazines? She walked slowly over to the couch and sank into it, hugging her knees to her chest, fingering the paper in her hand, wondering about the woman whose name she held, willing the name to come alive in the form of her mother.

She was still sitting there when the telephone rang again. It rang two or three times before registering in her thoughts. Shaking herself back into the present, she jumped up to answer it.

She was pleased to hear Jesselene's voice. "How are you today, dear?" she asked Elizabeth.

"Fine," she answered. "And you?"

"I'm having a great day. I just have a favor to ask you."

"Sure," she responded automatically. "What do you need?"

"The woman who was supposed to work this evening at TLC just called and said that her son came down with the chicken pox. I was wondering if you could work tonight."

"I guess so," Elizabeth said. "Paul said he would be home early." She hoped his headache would be better.

Then something occurred to Elizabeth. "Will you be there?"

"Well, that's one of the problems. You see, I could have

worked tonight but I'm expected at a church to give a presentation and plea for volunteers."

"Oh. I'd be by myself?" Elizabeth asked.

"I can be there for a little while, but I'm sure you'll do fine. Can you do it?"

Maybe it would do her good to get out of the house tonight and get her mind off the name on this paper. "Sure, I'd love to," she said. "I'll call Paul and make sure it's okay with him, but I'm sure that it will be."

"Wonderful," Jesselene said. "I'll see you there at seven."

Elizabeth hung up the phone and headed back for the couch, but Megan's cries stopped her. They sounded more like cries of pain than waking-up cries, and Elizabeth raced up the stairs wondering what a baby could do to get hurt in a crib.

When she finally reached the crib, she saw that Megan had only her little foot stuck between the crib rails. But Megan thought that was bad enough and sobbed in Elizabeth's arms.

As she soothed Megan, she realized how quickly her own problems of a moment before had vanished in the face of her daughter's needs. Suddenly she was not the daughter longing for a mother that she would probably never know, but she was the mother with so much to give to her own daughter. That was the role in which she had received so much happiness in the months since Megan's birth.

Paul was right—it was time that she gave up this unrealistic search for her past and concentrated on her future and what she could give her husband and child. Even if she found her mother, it wouldn't bring any more guarantee of happiness. She felt as if she could face the future with anticipation, even if it included Paul joining the Mormon church. She didn't completely understand it, but from what little she had felt when she had read the Book of Mormon that morning, she began to have a feeling for what attracted Paul to the Church.

She knew that she was not ready to tell Paul any of these things she was thinking—except maybe about her mother—because she was not yet ready to act upon any of these realizations. But maybe she could soon. The sunlight streamed through the window, warming Megan and her with its rays as if they were an affirmation of the newfound light within her. She felt closer to the peace that the missionaries had spoken of than she had ever felt before.

● ● ●

"So, do you feel confident enough for me to leave you?" Jesselene asked Elizabeth.

From behind the desk, Elizabeth looked at the neatly stacked papers and pamphlets and around the office with its comfortable furnishings and warm colors. Then there was the phone always near enough to call for help if there was a problem she felt incapable of handling.

"No," Elizabeth said, "I'm scared to death."

"You'll do just fine," Jesselene assured her. "You know where everything is, and if anyone needs counseling, make an appointment for tomorrow."

"You make it sound easy."

"Call me tomorrow, dear, and let me know how you did," Jesselene said. "Okay?"

"Okay."

Then she was alone. The first hour she answered the phone twice and was able to keep her wits about her to tell the callers what their hours were. She was just beginning to relax when the door opened and a very pregnant woman walked through the door. Oh no, was Elizabeth's first thought. She thinks we deliver babies, too.

But she didn't. What she wanted was a crib, but from

her manner and dress, she obviously needed other things when her baby came. Elizabeth filled out the necessary papers for her to borrow a crib and showed her what was available for the newborn baby. By the time she handled all that, Elizabeth felt a surge of confidence. She walked the woman to the door, squeezing her arm in a friendly gesture as she told her good-bye. "Let us know when the baby comes," she said. "We'll help you all we can."

The woman mumbled "thanks" and started down the hall. Elizabeth had almost shut the door when she noticed a young teenage girl, certainly no more than sixteen, huddled against a wall, her coat wrapped around her tightly against the chill in the hallway.

"Hi," Elizabeth said.

The girl merely smiled, making no attempt to come any closer. Elizabeth started to shut the door again, then it occurred to her that the only other office still open down the hall was an answering service. She poked her head out again and said, "Were you looking for the TLC office?"

The girl straightened up, pulling her coat even tighter around her. "I — I guess so," she said.

Elizabeth opened the door widely. "Come on in," she said warmly.

The girl looked toward the street, then back at Elizabeth as if deciding which direction she wanted to go. Elizabeth waited, then watched as she walked back toward the outside door, opened it, and waved to someone outside. Elizabeth saw the headlights of a car pass and caught a glimpse of a man driving. What she couldn't figure out was why this girl was sending her ride away. Her first problem, though, was to get the girl inside where she could talk to her and find out what she needed. "Come on in," she said again. "Would you like some hot chocolate?"

The girl slowly walked toward Elizabeth, carrying a bag that Elizabeth had not noticed before. As she passed Elizabeth through the door, Elizabeth noted that the girl's hair was pulled back into a neat French braid and that her clothes were the usual sweater and jeans of others her age. She was pretty but kept her eyes downcast until they got inside. Only when Elizabeth offered her a seat on the couch, did she look up with tear-filled eyes.

"I'm Elizabeth," Elizabeth said kindly. "Would you like some hot chocolate?"

"Yes," the girl said.

The water was already hot in the big stainless steel pot on the table in the corner, so Elizabeth busied herself with making the hot chocolate while her mind raced for the best way to befriend this girl so obviously in need of a friend. "I love your hair," she said, stirring away. "I've always been hopelessly clumsy at French-braiding my hair. Is it hard to do?"

"No," the girl said. "I do it myself."

"How long does that take?" She handed the girl her hot chocolate and sat down in the rocking chair close to the couch.

"Only about five minutes." She held onto her cup as if it were her only comfort.

Elizabeth took a deep breath, wondering why in the world she had ever wanted to work here because she felt so inadequate at the moment. She needed to find out the girl's name before going any farther. Maybe she could just ask her. "What's your name?" she asked.

"April Hill."

Easy enough. She'd test her luck and go on. "That's a pretty name for a pretty young girl. How old are you?"

"Sixteen." April's hot chocolate had cooled enough for her to take tiny sips of it. She avoided looking at Elizabeth.

"Is there some way we can help you?" Oh please, please, she pleaded inwardly. Please let it be something I know how to do.

145

Big tears began rolling down April's cheeks, two of them splashing into her hot chocolate. Everything Elizabeth had learned about counseling escaped her, but everything that Elizabeth knew of loneliness and sadness came flooding back. She put one arm around April, gently taking her cup and setting it on the coffee table with her other hand.

"Can you tell me about it?" she asked. "I'll help if I can."

"I'm pregnant," April said.

"Is that a real problem?" Elizabeth asked, then scolded herself silently. Sixteen and pregnant. Of course it's a problem. "Do you live at home with your parents?"

"I did," April said. She wiped her tears and took a deep breath, calming down enough so she could talk. "I lived with my mother and stepfather, but my stepfather says I can't stay there anymore unless I have . . . " She faltered. "You know."

"An abortion?"

"Yes," she said. "But I can't do it."

"Who brought you here?" Elizabeth asked. She thought back to the man she had seen in the car.

"My stepfather. My aunt told my mother that you would find a place for me to stay until she could talk to my stepfather." She looked up at Elizabeth with the first glimmer of hope in her eyes that Elizabeth had seen.

Why her? Of all the problems that had come through this door the last couple of weeks, this was the most serious, and she was probably the least capable of handling it. This was her chance to make a difference in someone's life, and all she could do was sit, her hands ice cold and her knees shaking, scared to death that she was going to blow it. She couldn't bring herself to tell the frightened girl that the plan to take girls into homes and care for them was just that—a plan.

"I'm sure we'll be able to help you, April," she said

finally. "And I'm sure your stepfather will come around in time, and we'll be able to work out a solution everyone can be happy with."

"Do you really think so?"

"I certainly do," Elizabeth said, displaying a confidence she didn't feel. "Now you go splash some water on that pretty face of yours. I'll make some phone calls, and we'll have you all taken care of. Okay?" Quickly she dialed Jesselene's number, hoping that by some miracle she had finished her program at the church and was already home. "You have reached the Mannings' number," Rowland's voice said. No miracle there.

Referring to the list of numbers taped to the desktop, she found the name of the vice-director of TLC, whom Elizabeth had never met. It rang four times, then "We are unable to come to the phone," a voice said. She slammed the phone down, then tiptoed over to the curtained glass separating the office from the waiting room and peeked out to see April fixing herself another cup of hot chocolate.

Jeanine. Maybe she could help Elizabeth decide what she should do. Oh please, please be home, Elizabeth pleaded silently. She was. As the child who answered went to get her mother, Elizabeth collapsed with relief in the chair. "Hello," she soon heard.

"Jeanine," she said immediately. "This is Elizabeth. You've got to help me."

"What's wrong?" she asked quickly. "Is it Megan?"

"No, no," Elizabeth said. She forced herself to calm down, realizing she had worried Jeanine. "Megan's fine. I'm at TLC, and I have a problem I don't know what to do about."

"I'll try to help," Jeanine said. "I'm no expert."

Elizabeth quickly told her about April, then waited, hoping for Jeanine to come up with a perfectly logical solution over which Elizabeth would kick herself for not having thought of it herself.

But she didn't. "I don't know," Jeanine said. "You certainly can't turn her away, but I haven't heard of any families ready to start accepting the girls into their homes yet. I guess you could bring her over here — for tonight at least."

Elizabeth considered that, appreciating Jeanine's offer, but the background noise coming from Jeanine's end of the phone sounded like a three-ring circus. It did not sound as if Jeanine needed anything else to deal with that night.

But it confirmed one thing to Elizabeth. If Jeanine could volunteer her home, overflowing with children, then Elizabeth could certainly take April home with her. The guest room had been ready for company for the six months since they had last had overnight guests. April could get a good night's sleep, and in the morning Jesselene would know what to do.

"Thanks, Jeanine," Elizabeth said. "It's sweet of you to offer, but I think it would be easier for me to take her home. You have enough people to take care of."

"I don't mind," Jeanine said.

"I know," Elizabeth said. "That's what's so great about you, but I have plenty of room for her. Thanks so much." Returning the phone to the hook, she folded her hands on the desk and thought about her decision. She felt good about it. She briefly considered calling Paul and asking his permission, but she didn't think he'd mind, and even if he did, she had no alternative anyway. I'll surprise him, she thought.

April sat huddled in the corner of the couch, sipping her hot chocolate, the tears gone, but the sad look still there. Elizabeth sat next to her, close enough to be friendly, far enough away not to be intimidating. "You're coming home with me tonight. I wasn't able to reach the director, so I decided that you can get a good night's sleep in my guest room. In the morning we'll call Mrs. Manning and see how we can best help you. Is that all right with you?"

"You don't mind?" April asked.

"We'd love to have you," Elizabeth said. "I have a nice husband and a sweet little baby who would just love to meet you."

"Really?" It was the first time that she had smiled and it warmed Elizabeth's heart.

"Really." Elizabeth patted her arm. "You finish your hot chocolate while I close up." April's eyes were a lot less sad than when Elizabeth had first seen her out in the hallway, and, turning off the lights, Elizabeth felt that her evening had been well spent. Helping girls like April was the whole reason for TLC, and Elizabeth was thrilled that she'd been able to solve this one particular dilemma. Selling houses had always been exciting to her, but working here made her feel worthwhile. "Let's go," she said to April, closing the door behind them.

About fifteen minutes later, Elizabeth pulled up into her driveway. "Wow," April said. "This is a beautiful house."

"Thanks." She put her car keys in her purse and looked up through the windshield to where April was looking. "We like living here. And there's plenty of room for you."

"I guess so," April said. "This is like staying at the Holiday Inn."

Elizabeth laughed appreciatively. "Now, that's an exaggeration."

Once in the house, Elizabeth snapped on the light, and April caught her breath. "Gosh, this is gorgeous."

"Thanks," Elizabeth said again. The downstairs was dark, so she knew that Paul had gone upstairs to wait for her. She took April upstairs and could hear the sound of the TV and see a faint light from their room. She'd wait until the morning for introductions.

April loved the guest room. "Gosh, even a TV." She sat down on the four-poster bed, forgetting her manners long enough to bounce up and down.

"And you don't need to be staying up tonight watching it," Elizabeth warned. She turned on the bathroom light. "You see if you need anything before you go to bed. I'll be back in a minute."

She was right—Paul was sitting up in bed with a book in hand and a movie in the VCR.

"Hi, how did things go at TLC?" he asked. "Did you handle everything okay? I thought I heard another voice."

"You did," she said. Then she hesitated. "I hope you won't be mad."

That got his attention. He put the book down. "Mad about what?"

She quickly told April's story in a whisper, ending with "So, is it okay with you if she spends a night or two?"

He looked more amazed than anything as she spoke, then broke into a wide smile. "It's fine with me, sweetheart. I'm proud of you, and I'm glad you're so interested in this."

"Yeah," she said. "I'm sort of proud of me, too."

"Should I get up and meet her now?"

"No, that can wait until the morning, I think. She's really tired." She leaned across the bed to kiss him. "I'll be back as soon as I get April settled."

"Okay," he said. He opened his book again but called her before she walked into the hall. "Oh, Bets?"

"What?"

His smile turned a little sheepish. "The missionaries called tonight and wanted to know if they could come and teach another discussion tomorrow night. Is that okay with you?"

"Do I have to feed them again?"

"No."

"Okay, then," After all, this was the new Elizabeth.

She found April experimenting with the touch-on light. "This is neat," April said.

"Glad you like it. Did you find everything you need?"

"More than enough."

Elizabeth turned back the comforter. "Now don't stay up too late. You have a little baby to think about now. You both need your rest."

April's hand instinctively went to rest on her stomach. "I know. I never forget it's there."

"You won't," Elizabeth said. "Pretty soon he, or she, will be kicking you so hard that you wouldn't be able to forget even if you wanted to."

"Where's your husband?" April suddenly asked, fear on her face. "Was he mad about me being here?"

"No," Elizabeth assured her. "He was glad to have you. He'll meet you in the morning. Now get some sleep. It's getting late."

"Yes, ma'am."

As Elizabeth walked to the door, April called out, "Elizabeth?"

"Yes?" She turned back.

"Thank you."

"You're welcome, dear. I'm glad I could help."

I wish someone had helped Karen Lassiter when she needed help, Elizabeth thought as she walked down the hall to her bedroom. But as she faced herself in the bathroom mirror, she remembered her vow earlier that day. The past is behind you, she told herself. Karen Lassiter was the mother of another Elizabeth. And this Elizabeth in this bathroom mirror made a difference in someone's life tonight. And it felt good.

Jesselene put down her telephone receiver. She was so surprised at her conversation with Elizabeth that she sat down at her kitchen table to think about it. A couple of weeks ago, just on an impulse, she had asked Elizabeth to help with TLC occasionally, never even considering that she might make room in her busy life to get very involved. And now, Elizabeth had taken into her home a young girl in need who by coincidence had come into the office when Elizabeth was there. Plus, they had shown up in church the Sunday before.

Was it really coincidence, or could she see in her own life, as she had so many times before, the hand of the Lord bringing about his purpose and will? And what was her role in it?

She shook herself out of these thoughts, quieting herself to listen carefully that day and to be willing to be used as the Lord might wish. For now, her plans were already set. She had told Elizabeth that she would be over within the hour to counsel with April and determine her needs.

When Jesselene arrived, Elizabeth and April were at the

coffee table in the den playing Scrabble. "Oh, I love to play Scrabble," Jesselene said. Smiling at April, she took a seat beside her on the couch and wrestled several letter tiles away from Megan.

"It isn't easy playing with a baby," Elizabeth said.

"I remember," Jesselene said.

"April, this is Jesselene, the woman I told you about," Elizabeth said.

"Hi," April said self-consciously. She glanced up only briefly before turning her attention back to the Scrabble board.

"Would you like me to take Megan while you two finish your game?" Jesselene asked. But with one successful sweep of her arm, Megan totalled out the Scrabble board, sending letters everywhere.

April laughed, and Elizabeth moaned, reaching for the tiles before Megan could put one in her mouth. "I think our game just ended," she said. "I was losing anyway."

Jesselene took Megan and bounced her on her lap while April and Elizabeth picked up the game. "Don't you just love Elizabeth's home?" Jesselene asked conversationally.

"Yes, I love it," April said enthusiastically. "It was like staying in a hotel."

"Thank you," Elizabeth said. "Megan and I will leave you two alone to talk."

April's hands were shaking in her lap as she stared down at them. Jesselene put her own hand over April's and patted them kindly.

"April," she said. "I'm not here to judge you or lecture you. I'm here to make sure that you and your baby are taken care of and have the best future possible. You've already made a wonderful decision to choose life for your baby." April's hands had calmed down. "So will you let us help you and your baby?"

April looked up with such a sad look in her eyes that

Jesselene wanted to take her in her arms. "Yes, ma'am," she said. "I'm not a bad person. Really."

"Of course, you aren't, dear," Jesselene said. "And don't let anyone tell you that you are." Then she put her arm around April. "Now let's look at the options."

A short time later, Elizabeth looked up from feeding Megan when Jesselene and April walked into the kitchen, Jesselene's arm firmly around April. "I think everything's going to be fine," Jesselene said. "I'm going to call April's mother first of all and let her know where she is and that she's okay. Then we'll get her back in school as soon as possible for as long as possible. Then, we'll see that she gets to a doctor to make sure that she's okay."

"I'd be glad to take her," Elizabeth said. She washed off Megan's hands and face as she spoke, then unbuckled her from her high chair. "Let me take Megan upstairs and put her down for a nap," she said. "Then we can talk."

April walked over to Elizabeth and held her hands out for Megan. "Let me put her in her bed, please."

Megan fell into April's arms. "Well," Elizabeth said, "since it's okay with her, I guess it's okay with me. Just make sure she has her blankie, or it will be another trip upstairs."

"Okay," April said. "Let's go find blankie, Megan."

They left laughing as Jesselene and Elizabeth sat down. "She's a sweet girl," Elizabeth said.

"Yes," Jesselene said. She hoped she appeared more professional and collected than she really felt. When she had first come into the den and had seen the scared look in April's eyes, it was like looking at herself in a mirror so many years ago. It was the first time she had dealt with a young girl in the same situation that she had been in—scared, bereft of the support of her parents, too young for the decisions she had to make. She could feel it all again so clearly. It was the very situation Rowland wanted her to avoid. She suddenly realized that Elizabeth had asked her something. "Pardon me?"

"What are you doing the rest of the day?" she asked again.

"Nothing too exciting," she answered. Her thoughts had distracted her, and she needed to speak to Elizabeth before April came back into the room. "How did it work out having April here last night?"

"Fine, I guess," Elizabeth said. "She really wasn't here that long."

"Do you think she could stay here a couple more days while I make arrangements for her to stay somewhere else?" she asked. "We really don't have this part of our program organized yet."

"We'd love to have her stay," Elizabeth said.

Jesselene looked closely but could only see sincerity in Elizabeth's eyes.

●　●　●

April had proved to be enjoyable company for Elizabeth that day. She was smart and could hold her own in a discussion on books, current events, or most anything else they had talked about. Having gotten her number from Jesselene, Mrs. Hill had called that afternoon, talking to her for quite a while. After that, April had seemed more relaxed and less preoccupied. She was quick to offer to help with jobs around the house, and Megan already adored her.

The missionaries rode up into the driveway that evening as Paul pulled up in his Mercedes. "Hi, Sister Danforth," both missionaries called out, climbing off their bikes and blowing on their cold hands.

"Hi, Elder Thorne. Hi, Elder Harrison." Holding the door open in the chilly night air, she shook the missionaries' cold hands. She should have picked them up while April watched Megan.

Paul followed the missionaries into the kitchen, pecking Elizabeth on the cheek as he passed. "Hi, Bets," he said. "Where's the baby?"

Just then April walked into the kitchen, carrying a damp-haired Megan who squealed with delight when she saw her daddy.

"Hi," April said shyly, holding onto the wiggly baby.

"Hello." Paul took Megan from April and smiled at her.

"You're Mormon missionaries, aren't you?" April asked the missionaries.

Oh no, Elizabeth thought, not another one.

"Sure are," Elder Thorne said. He introduced them both.

"One of my friends is a Mormon, and I've seen you riding your bikes around town," April explained.

Paul was already herding everyone into the den. He must be excited about hearing what they had to say tonight. April followed, having no trouble talking to the missionaries as they listed all the high-school Mormons they knew.

Elizabeth was the last to enter the room and noticed that the men had taken the same seats they had during the previous lesson. Only April and Elizabeth stood closer to a door than to a chair, and Elizabeth was determined to use the door before she used a chair that night.

"You can sit here, Elizabeth," Paul said, pointing to the couch beside him. "April, if you'd like to stay, you're welcome to. We've been taking some lessons about the Mormon church."

Elizabeth spoke quickly, putting her hand through April's arm. "That's okay. I need to get Megan to bed, and April and I have a Scrabble tournament going." She avoided Paul's eyes as she spoke since she knew that they would be filled with disappointment. With April there that day, it had been easy to resist the temptation to pick up the Book of Mormon. If she stayed away from the discussion, maybe she could go back to the spiritual apathy she had gotten used to over the years. That she could handle; it was all those feelings these Mormons stirred up she couldn't.

"Please, Elizabeth," Paul asked gently. She risked looking at him. His disappointment tugged at her heart. "April can either stay or watch TV in the bedroom," he added.

April looked like she wanted to stay, but Elizabeth didn't give her a chance. "Not tonight, Paul," she said. "There's a cake when you're finished."

She picked Megan up from the floor and walked out of the room, April following. Elder Thorne looked disappointed when she passed by them, but Elder Harrison managed a smile and reached out to touch the baby's hand.

With Megan tucked into bed, Elizabeth walked past April's room and found her lying across the bed watching a game show. "Did you want to play Scrabble?" she asked.

"I don't think so," she answered. "I think I feel a little sick."

She did look pale. Elizabeth walked into the bathroom and came back with a cold damp washcloth, which she folded and handed to April. "This might help," she said. "Would you like something to drink?"

April turned up her nose. "I don't think so. I'll be okay in a minute."

Pulling the rocking chair up closer to the bed, Elizabeth sat down. "Do you mind if I stay?" she asked.

"No." She took a couple of deep breaths and put the cold cloth on her forehead. "Can I ask you something?"

"Sure," Elizabeth said. She still remembered plenty about nausea. But, surprisingly, that wasn't what April wanted to know.

"Don't you like the Mormon church?" she asked.

April was either very perceptive, or Elizabeth was more

obvious than she had thought. "Well," she said, wondering if she could explain how she really felt. "It's not that I don't like the Mormon church—I've just never been interested in any church. Some people just aren't, you know."

"Does your husband like it?"

"Yes, he does."

"Will that make you mad?"

"You certainly are inquisitive tonight," Elizabeth said. She got up and walked over to sit down next to April. She realized that April was just young and curious and had no idea what a touchy subject religion was to discuss around this house. Or at least had been.

"I'm sorry," April said. "I didn't mean to be nosey."

"No, that's all right. Why are you so interested anyway?"

"I don't know," she answered. "I knew some Mormon kids and they always did the neatest things at their churches. I went home with some once, and they had eight kids. I just thought that was neat. I always wanted my Mom to have more kids before they got divorced."

She sounded sad again. Elizabeth turned the cloth on her forehead over to the cooler side. "I'm sorry," Elizabeth said. Sorry she was sick, sorry she was alone, sorry she'd never had the brothers and sisters she'd wanted. Maybe sorry too that she wasn't more interested in the Mormon church if that would make April any happier that evening.

"And I like that woman that came today," April continued.

"Jesselene? I do too."

"If I could be like her, I'd join the Mormon church too," April said earnestly.

Elizabeth hadn't considered the situation from that point of view. She had thought that Jesselene would be Jesselene even if she wasn't a Mormon and that Jeanine would be Jeanine if she wasn't a Mormon. But maybe they were the people they were because of their church. They all seemed to have something appealing in common—like a purpose or reason to live or something, the something that Elizabeth never had enough of in her life.

While Elizabeth was considering this, April pulled the afghan over her and closed her eyes. "I'm so tired," she said.

"You rest then," Elizabeth said. "Call me if you need me—I'll be downstairs." She pulled the afghan over April's feet and walked out, closing the door softly behind her.

She tried reading a magazine in her bedroom, but, after a half an hour or so, she tiptoed out into the hallway and sat down on the top stair where she listened to the hum of the voices in the den. It would be so easy to get up and walk down into the den as she had hundreds of times before. Then she could announce that, yes, she had read part of the Book of Mormon and, yes, it seemed sensible enough to her. Then, after she picked Paul up off the floor, she could say that she needed something in her life, and she thought that it was whatever the missionaries and the rest of their Mormon friends had. Would they teach her too?

She buried her face in her hands. It sounded so simple. Why was it so hard? Was her bargain with God still so important?

"Bets, are you all right?" Paul was standing at the bottom of the stairs, looking up at her.

She jerked her head up. "Sure," she said. "Just tired. Are you finished?"

"Yes." He walked up the stairs and sat down beside her, putting his arm around her. "They wanted to know when I wanted to be baptized. I said a week from Sunday." He waited.

All she could think of to say was "So?"

"So, they said okay. I could go to church this Sunday and have the rest of the discussions next week. Is that okay?"

She put her head on his shoulder. "That's fine, honey, if it will make you happy."

"It will, Bets." He took her chin in his hand and tipped her head back to look into her eyes. "Maybe it could make you happy, too. If you'd just give it a chance."

"Maybe it would, Paul. Maybe it would," she said suddenly, without thinking first. She regretted getting his hopes up.

That must have startled him, his eyes widening as they looked at her. Too late, she thought. I shouldn't get his hopes up. She jumped up before he could say anything else. "I guess the missionaries are ready for their cake," she said. She pulled him up from the stair by his hand. "You go ask them what they want to drink." She hopped down the stairs, leaving him to stare after her.

Late that night, as Elizabeth rubbed lotion into her hands, she said, "The missionaries didn't stay very long tonight." She made sure the alarm was set before she got into bed. Paul already lay there reading.

"They had to go administer to someone in the hospital."

Pulling the covers up to her chin, she tried to figure that one out. "They're administrators at the hospital?" was the closest she could get.

But Paul laughed, so evidently they weren't. "No," he said. "They were going to go the hospital to see someone who is sick and anoint his head with oil and say a prayer to make him well. It's called administering."

"How do you know all this?" she asked.

"They explained it to me," he said. "Plus, I've been reading."

"Mmmm," she said very noncommittally, but she thought how the Mormons were full of surprises. Imagine — curing people on faith, and in the twentieth century too.

CHAPTER

18

Before he even reached the bottom of the stairs the next morning, Paul could hear that more than usual was happening in the kitchen for that time of the day. He picked out three female voices, one of which was his wife's pleading with his daughter to hurry up and eat. He walked into the kitchen to find April eating a bowl of Cheerios and Jesselene playing airplane with Megan and her oatmeal. Bets was standing in front of the half-unloaded dishwasher, looking frustrated. "What's happening in here?" he asked.

"Good morning, honey," Elizabeth said.

"Hello, Paul," Jesselene said.

"Hi, Mr. Manning," April said.

"We're trying to get ready to take April to school," Elizabeth explained, "but Megan isn't eating."

Jesselene smiled. "I'm sort of interfering. I know Elizabeth can handle taking April to school, but I decided to tag along."

"Oh, no," Elizabeth said, "I'm glad to have you. You know more about dealing with high school counselors than I do."

"I'm sure Bets is glad you came," Paul said. "I don't know what she'd talk about if she didn't talk about you."

Elizabeth blushed, and Jesselene looked pleased. "You two are sweet."

Paul sat down opposite April and reached for the Cheerios. He hadn't really said much to April since she had been there. In fact, he had thought she would have been gone by now, but since she wasn't, maybe it was time he had a conversation with her. "Are you feeling better this morning, April?" he asked.

"Yes sir," she said. She chased her last Cheerio around the bowl and scooped it up before she looked up at him. When she did, it was with frank admiration in her eyes. "You're a lawyer?" she asked. "I'd love to be a lawyer. It must be exciting."

"Sometimes it can be," he said. She seemed like a nice enough girl. "I can talk to you about law school if you'd like." He could understand why Bets would want to help a young girl with big brown eyes that hinted of loneliness and who was obviously in awe of sharing a box of Cheerios with a lawyer.

"April, do you have any books you need to take to school?" Elizabeth asked. "We'd better be leaving."

"I think we'd better give up on the oatmeal," Jesselene said. She tore a piece of toast in half and tried to give it to Megan, but Megan pushed it away.

Elizabeth felt her forehead. "I hope she isn't getting sick. She usually eats."

"She wants her daddy to feed her," Paul said. Sure enough, he slid a spoonful of Cheerios right into her mouth. "How long are you going to be gone?"

Jesselene and Elizabeth looked at each other. "I don't know," Elizabeth said. "No more than a hour, I'm sure. Why?"

"You can leave her here with me while you go," he said. "I've got some work I can do at home."

Elizabeth pushed the high chair closer to him immediately. "One problem solved," she said. "Now I'll go make sure that April is ready and do something to my hair." She ran her hand through her hair and sighed. "I feel like I'm starting high school all over again."

"Everything will be fine," Jesselene said. Elizabeth hurried from the room as they laughed at her.

"She reminds me a lot of my daughter, Diane," Jesselene commented.

"They look a lot alike, too," Paul said. "Both beautiful, of course."

"Of course." Jesselene started to clear the table as he alternately fed himself and Megan. "They do look alike," she said thoughtfully, "and Diane's baby pictures look just like Megan. Maybe we'll find out we're related back a few generations."

"Maybe so," Paul said. He glanced at the door to make sure Bets hadn't come back in, then lowered his voice. "I'm going to be baptized next Sunday."

"Oh, Paul, that's wonderful." She too looked over toward the door. "What about Elizabeth?"

"She isn't the least bit interested yet," he said regretfully.

"Do you know why? Maybe I could help if I knew what her problem is."

Glancing back at the door, expecting Bets to appear any minute, he shook his head. "It has a lot to do with how she grew up. She feels like God let her down because she never had a real family."

Jesselene shook her head. "That's a tough one." Elizabeth and April were heard coming down the stairs. "Maybe I can talk to her, though," Jesselene said quickly.

"Thanks." He looked over with a big smile as Elizabeth came into the room. "Gorgeous, as usual, sweetheart," he said. "You too, April. You look real nice." That brought a big smile to April's face.

Paul finished feeding Megan her cereal as he watched, and listened, to the three women walking out the door to the car. Jesselene was just the motherly type that Bets needed in her life.

"Finished, babe?" He wiped Megan's sticky hands before he lifted her out of the high chair and put her down into the playpen. Then he surveyed the kitchen. He could do a lot of work in there if he decided to. "What do you think, Megan? Do you think that Daddy could help a little bit with this mess?"

She didn't try to dissuade him, as he had hoped, so he started unloading the dishwasher. Nephi had suggested that the best way to interest Bets in the church would be by the example he set, and he was determined that nothing would change between them because of his decision. In fact, he was going to try twice as hard to be a good husband and father and show her that the gospel could only make things better in their life. From the first time he had heard about temples and their purpose, he knew what his goal was — to go there with Bets and Megan one day. And if cleaning up the kitchen would help, then clean up the kitchen it would be.

●　●　●

Taking April back to school turned out to be easier than she had expected. Elizabeth had been far more nervous than April, who seemed to have steeled herself to face any possible embarrassment. The principal had warmly welcomed April back and eased their minds considerably.

On the way back to the BMW, Jesselene said, "Elizabeth, dear."

Elizabeth knew that they were about to have a serious

conversation. Elizabeth hoped it was something she didn't mind having a serious conversation about. "Yes?" she said.

"I know this is none of my business, but I've grown to love you and Paul the last few weeks, almost as if you were my children." She hesitated. "So can I ask you something?"

"Sure," Elizabeth said. She warmed under the expression of love and couldn't think of any question that Jesselene could ask that she would mind answering. By now, they had reached the car and were standing while they talked. Elizabeth motioned for Jesselene to get in. They both settled comfortably on the seats of the automobile.

"Is there a particular reason you're not interested in the Church?" Jesselene asked.

Except maybe that question.

"If it's anything that I could help you with, I will gladly do it," Jesselene said kindly.

Elizabeth didn't answer at first. "It's a long story," she said at last.

"You've said that before," Jesselene said. "And one time I felt as if you were about to tell me. But you stopped for some reason."

"I know. I did. But I just don't share my past with many people."

"I'm sorry if it was that painful. Maybe it would help if you shared it with me."

Her smile was so kind, her hand over Elizabeth's so gentle as she leaned forward that Elizabeth lowered her guard. She wanted Jesselene to take her past, explain it to her so somehow it finally made some sense, and give it back to her without the pain. So she told her about her lonely childhood, starting with her adoptive parents who had both died shortly after the adoption. Perhaps another day, she could start even farther back with the mother who had abandoned her, but for now that was still too much.

Jesselene listened without comment until Elizabeth

stopped. "I'm so sorry that you had such an unhappy childhood," she said. "But you have such a wonderful husband and child now."

"I know," Elizabeth said. "I do."

"But the Church could bring you so much happiness," Jesselene said. "You have a family, an eternal family. I think, no, I know, you would find the peace and comfort you have always wanted."

Elizabeth sighed. It sounded exactly like what she wanted.

"And, besides," Jesselene added, "it's true. No matter what you or anyone else decides about it, it is true. And in the acceptance of that truth, you can find a tremendous freedom and happiness. Paul has already found it."

"I know. And I envy him for it."

"But it can be yours too." Leaning forward, Jesselene squeezed Elizabeth's hand.

"I think I know that. But . . ."

"But what?" Jesselene asked after Elizabeth's long pause.

"I always blamed God for taking my family away from me," she said slowly. "I made a bargain with him that I would believe in him when I had a real family. And I never did, so I always figured that he didn't need my love."

Jesselene looked so troubled that Elizabeth was afraid she had said something awful against her beliefs. Jesselene's voice trembled as she spoke. "Oh Elizabeth, my heart aches for you, but that was your bargain, not God's. He wants you to be happy with or without parents. But you can't hold your past against him, Elizabeth. It had its purpose however hard it is for you to accept."

"Do you really think so?"

"I know so," Jesselene said. She watched Elizabeth thoughtfully for a moment. "Has your way brought you happiness?"

Elizabeth was just as thoughtful. "Not really," she admitted.

• • •

Paul had cleaned the kitchen thoroughly, even washing the counters and mopping the floor. He was picking Megan up out of the playpen when he heard the BMW pull into the driveway. Oh no, he had forgotten something. Plopping Megan back down in the playpen, which broke her little heart, he ran into the den.

He picked up the Book of Mormon from his desk and thought for a moment, then lined it up so that its back lay on the scratch that Megan had made with his car keys the week before. Ever since he had discovered the Book of Mormon moved from where he had laid it on the magazines, he had been sure that Bets had been reading it. Especially after her comment about repentance the night before. If she picked it up today, the scratch would tell.

By the time Bets reached the patio, he and Megan, her tears dried, met her at the door. He wrapped her and Megan in a hug before she could even see the clean kitchen. There was no doubt about it—he felt wonderful.

The day of Paul's baptism was beautifully cold and clear. Elizabeth lay in bed and watched the last few leaves on the tree outside their bedroom window dance in the breeze. She didn't dread the day because Paul was going to be baptized—she felt that she had come to grips with that well enough. She was more afraid that she would feel like the proverbial fifth wheel. She already knew from previous re-actions that every Mormon they met would be thrilled about Paul joining their church. And there she would be, tagging along. She could hear the introduction now. Paul would say, "Have you met my wife? No, she isn't a member of the Church. She doesn't like religion." Maybe she could stay home.

Paul stirred beside her, so she knew he was waking up. Rolling over, she shook his shoulder. "Paul, do I have to go today?"

"Go where?" he mumbled.

"To church and your baptism."

His eyes flew open. "That's right. It's Sunday morning."

"Yes, it's the morning that I lose my husband." She

stared at him, already regretting her words. Now why did she say that?

He slipped his arm around her. "You don't lose me today, Bets. You will never lose me." His arm tightened. "In fact, one of the teachings I like most is that we can be married for eternity."

"You're assuming a lot," she said with a smile.

"No, I'm hoping for a lot." He swung his legs out of bed. Sitting on the edge of the bed, he looked back at her sadly. "You don't have to go if you don't want to, Bets. But I'll miss you. And," he added as he stood up, "this is not the day you lose your husband. This is the day that I become an even better husband to you and a better father to Megan."

Elizabeth's eyes filled with tears as Paul closed the bathroom door behind him. No way would she miss this big day in his life — she knew Paul would never let her feel left out. She jumped out of bed and went to bang on the bathroom door. "Hey, hurry up in there," she said. "I've got to get ready for church."

About two hours and fifteen minutes later, they were pulling into the church parking lot. April was with them, too. She had called her mother for permission. Quite a few cars were already there when they arrived, and once again the missionaries greeted them. Walking into the chapel, April recognized several of her friends from school and waved to them.

Even Elizabeth felt comfortable being there. She was beginning to put some names with some faces and listened attentively when the bishop announced Paul's baptism and expressed the pleasure of everyone at the good news. Another pang — of envy perhaps — pinched her heart.

However, Megan started crying so loudly during the first hymn that Elizabeth squeezed past everyone on the row and took her out. She actually felt some regret that she would miss part of the meeting. After several minutes alone in the spacious foyer, Megan finally hushed. Elizabeth listened to the sacrament prayers over the intercom and the quietness that followed them. She felt a peace start as a warm spot in her heart and spread throughout her whole body. Then as coughs and whispers signaled the end of the sacrament, the chapel doors opened, and Jesselene came out carrying a fussy little baby.

Megan roused up as Jesselene came over. "His mother and daddy have to give a talk, so I volunteered to babysit," Jesselene explained. "But he wasn't very happy about it."

"Megan was fussy too," Elizabeth said.

"Poor baby." Jesselene rubbed Megan's head with her free hand. "There are a couple of rocking chairs back in the nursery. Let's go back there, and you can rock her."

Elizabeth followed her to the nursery, and they both settled into chairs, resting the babies on their laps and rocking slowly. Both babies soon quieted, and the two women listened to the talks over the speaker. It seemed to Elizabeth that the whole room was filled with peace.

Megan woke up whimpering slightly as the strains of the closing hymn began. The two women looked at each other, a warmth flowing around and between them and filling the nursery with a soft love.

"Thank you," Elizabeth said for no particular reason as she got up. Her voice quivered with emotion. Jesselene looked at her a little quizzically but wisely said no more. She hugged Elizabeth as best she could with one arm before she left the room. Elizabeth stood for a while in the nursery until she could hear footsteps in the hallway, then said, "Let's go find Daddy. He's probably wondering where we are."

Elizabeth found Paul in the chapel, surrounded by people wishing him well. He was smiling and obviously excited, but she could see that he was also very serious. Maybe he was as nervous about his baptism as she would be. Maybe if she saw his baptism and found out everything she could about it, then she wouldn't be nervous if she were ever baptized. Then again, maybe if she were baptized, her life wouldn't always be such a conflict of maybes.

● ● ●

Paul slipped into the front pew beside Bets after changing into his baptismal clothes. He automatically put his arm around her. Her smile seemed a bit stoic as she fed Megan Cheerios from a Tupperware bowl. "I love you," he whispered into her ear. He felt sorry for her because he knew, even if the others didn't, that she was very uncomfortable sitting there waiting for him to be baptized. She patted him on the knee but didn't answer him.

Bets joined him on the opening hymn, which was "Come Follow Me," while Megan banged on the hymnbook. As Paul listened to the opening prayer that Jesselene gave and the short talk on baptism by Rowland, he didn't feel the burning within him that he had felt while reading the Book of Mormon. There was instead a presence in the room that he couldn't deny, a sweetness that made breathing hurt and that filled his eyes with tears. This was what he had searched for all his life.

Unconsciously he squeezed Bets's shoulders before he stood up to follow the missionaries to the font. He looked up at Bets as he walked down into the water. Drawn by his eyes, she looked up from Megan and smiled at him—a genuine smile with the slightest nod of her head. The room and people around him seemed to fade into the background as Elder Harrison reminded Paul to bend his knees as the missionary dipped him backwards. Everything he felt and heard in the font—from the prayer to the gentle slapping of the warm water—was intense and clear.

The water washed over him, but he didn't struggle. He came up and thought that he breathed in the sweetest air he had ever breathed. He eyes shifted from the witnesses who nodded their approval to the only person he could easily recognize in the room — Bets. She smiled again over Megan's head, but it was a resigned kind of smile, and she turned her attention back to a fussy Megan.

Paul dressed as quickly as he could, exchanging small talk with Elder Harrison that seemed a bit unreal after what he had just experienced. When he returned to the room, Bets was standing against the wall with Megan, rocking back and forth. He walked over to her, putting his hand on Megan's back. "Are you okay?" he asked.

"Sure," she answered, burying her face in Megan's hair.

Paul returned to his seat. After Nephi's talk on the gift of the Holy Ghost, the missionaries motioned for him to sit in the chair they had moved up front. Several men quickly surrounded him and stacked their hands on his head. In front of him to the right, he could hear Megan begin to cry. He smiled. She probably didn't know what they were doing to her daddy. The weight of the hands pressed upon his head, and Elder Thorne began the prayer. Then, Paul could feel nothing but his words burning their way into his heart: "And we bless you, Brother Danforth, that the spirituality and example of your life will bring those you love in your family closer to an understanding of the truth that you have so readily embraced."

Bets, he means Bets, was all Paul could think. She will know for herself one day. Nothing Elder Thorne could have said would have made him happier.

The prayer over, he shook hands all around the circle. Bets had left the room, and he could hear Megan still crying in the hallway. Paul sat down, and the baptismal meeting ended with Jeanine's prayer. After the final amen, people began to crowd around him to shake his hand and congratulate him. He was happy and gracious but anxious to find Bets. As soon as he felt it was proper, Paul shook the missionaries' hands once again and excused himself.

Bets was out in the hall. As soon as Megan saw Paul, she stretched out her arms to be taken. He lifted his daughter from her mother's arms and hugged her. Megan stopped crying and gave a shaky laugh, patting his neck. He shifted her to one arm, then hugged Bets with the other. Was he mistaken, or did Bets's eyes seem to glisten with tears?

"Congratulations, honey," Bets said. Behind her were Jesselene and another woman.

"You sure have a wonderful wife, Brother Danforth," the other woman commented.

"Thank you." He shook her extended hand, then she told Bets and Jesselene good-bye and walked away.

"You all right, sweetheart?" he asked Bets.

Jesselene put her arm around Bets's waist. "She's just fine," Jesselene said. "I've been babysitting with them."

He looked at Bets. She looked awfully tired. It must have been a long day for her, struggling with Megan.

"Honey, I really am happy for you," Bets said. "Don't worry."

Jesselene reached up to give him a hug. "Congratulations, Paul," she said.

Maybe he should have said something spiritual and inspired for their first conversation after his wonderful baptism, but all he could think to say as he reached down to pick up the diaper bag at Bets's feet was "I'm starving. Do we have anything to eat at home?"

Walking down the hallway, he reflected that there was plenty of time to be spiritual and inspired. Today was just the beginning.

20

Once again Elizabeth picked up the copy of the Book of Mormon in the den and settled into the chair to read. The past four days since Paul's baptism, it had become a regular routine with her. In fact, the overall routine that had developed at their home was very pleasant. The feeling of separation that she had feared might happen never materialized. Paul was so content and peaceful. She had never seen him happier.

Paul had begun taking April to school before leaving for work, and Elizabeth spent her mornings with Megan and housework before handling what few real-estate appointments she had. She was usually finished in plenty of time to come home and read, then pick April up from school and be home before Megan began to miss her. April always wanted to play with Megan for a while, and Elizabeth invariably went back to the den to read the Book of Mormon some more.

In a way that she didn't understand, her time with the book had become the focal point of her day. One time, Paul had picked up the Book of Mormon where she had left it lying on the coffee table. Elizabeth had used a rattle as the bookmark, and it fell out noisily. Although he looked at her questioningly, he didn't say anything. Another day, she ventured to ask him two questions—one about faith and one about forgiveness. He was startled but thrilled and answered with a zest that surprised her. She hoped he wasn't getting his hopes too high.

She had been reading about some awful destructions recently. Today she was starting 3 Nephi 11. As she read about the visit of Christ to the Nephites, the verses awakened in her the remembrance of half-forgotten and poorly learned Sunday School lessons from her youth. These verses gave a portrayal of a Savior she had never understood from those long-ago lessons. Her heart opened up to what she read, and she felt no longer able to shut it out. That afternoon, as she closed the Book of Mormon, she knew suddenly that she believed it, not remembering a specific moment or verse that had convinced her, just feeling the warmth and brilliance of the truth she had read.

But even as she realized that she believed, she wondered what she was going to do with that knowledge. As Jesselene had said, it was true whether or not she lived it, and she still wasn't sure she was ready to change her life. It was such a tremendous decision—could it be based on merely a feeling?

The questions raced around and around in her mind until she glanced at the clock and saw that she was already later than usual leaving to pick April up. She sighed. The questions would just have to wait.

● ● ●

April was sitting on the low wall that surrounded the front of the school when Elizabeth arrived. She walked slower than usual to the car, clutching her books to her chest, and she looked pale. Elizabeth hoped April hadn't caught the flu that had been going around the school.

Elizabeth reached over to open the door for April. "Are you all right?" she asked. "You look pale."

April fell back against the seat. "My stomach started cramping in the last class."

"Badly?"

"Not real bad, I guess."

Elizabeth forced herself to remain calm. "Let's get you home and to bed," she said evenly. "Maybe you were just on your feet too much today."

When they pulled into the driveway, she turned casually to April, who was gathering her books up. "Are you bleeding any?"

"I don't think so," April said. "Why? Do you think it's something serious?"

"I doubt it," she answered lightly. "But maybe we can check with the doctor if you don't feel better in a little bit."

April went up to her room with strict orders from Elizabeth to get into bed and be still. Elizabeth quickly settled Megan into the playpen with a bottle. When she got up to April's room, she found her in bed, looking even paler. "How do you feel?" she asked.

"I am bleeding," April said quietly. Her eyes were wide with fright, and Elizabeth could see that her hands were shaking.

Squeezing April's hands that clutched the covers tightly, Elizabeth tried to sound confident. "That happens sometimes. Why don't I call Dr. Simmons and see what he says?"

After she reached the doctor, he spoke with April for several minutes asking her questions that she answered in such a scared voice that Elizabeth sat on the bed beside her and held her hand for support. "He told me to stay in bed with my feet up all night," she said when she hung up.

"And if it's no better in the morning, to call his office and come in to see him."

"Then that's what you'll do. We'll treat you like a queen and serve you supper in bed. Okay?"

"Okay." She tried a little smile. "He said it's not unusual."

"Well, he's right. We just need to make sure we do what he says. I'll go get you some magazines and juice, and you lie back and try not to worry."

April nodded her head. "Thanks."

After she reached the hallway outside April's door, she let the worry clutch her heart. April had become like a daughter to her the past few weeks, and she didn't want anything to happen to her. This was one of the reasons she had been reluctant to get involved with TLC in the first place. She had been afraid that she would get attached to the people she helped and leave herself open to all sorts of pain when things didn't work out the way she wanted them to. A month ago she hadn't even known April, and now she was scared for her.

But she couldn't let April see it, so she fixed orange juice and took up a glass to her, then talked cheerfully about the cute things that Megan had done that day. April seemed to appreciate it, finally smiling again and settling back on the pillow as Elizabeth turned on the TV to a Brady Bunch rerun.

When Elizabeth checked on April for the last time before going to bed herself, April felt no better. But at least she hadn't gotten any worse either. Closing April's door behind her and insisting that she call her if she needed her during the night, Elizabeth went back to their bedroom. Paul was reading what looked like an awfully dry law book. He looked up.

"How is she? Any better?"

"About the same. I hope she'll be all right." Actually

it was about the fifth time Paul had asked those two questions that evening and about the fifth time she'd said those same words. He had even gone in to talk to April for about an hour, relating some of the difficult cases he had handled. She had listened wide-eyed.

"She'll be okay," he said. "You're taking good care of her." He put his book down to pat the pillow beside him. "You look awfully tired, though. Why don't you lie down and get some sleep? Everything will be better in the morning."

He was right—she was awfully tired. Lying down, she tried to remember the last time she had sat down that day, but couldn't. Surely April would be better in the morning.

"You're right. It'll be better in the morning," she mumbled sleepily to Paul. "Good-night."

CHAPTER

21

April was not better in the morning—she was much worse. When Elizabeth walked into her room, she was trying to get back into bed, crying from pain and fright. Elizabeth helped her into bed, said a few words to try to calm her down, then called for Paul.

He came quickly. "What's wrong?" he asked.

Elizabeth clutched his arm. "I think we need to get her to the hospital. I'm going to call the doctor and Jesselene to meet me there. Can you help her down to the car?"

"Sure." He went swiftly over to the bed, but when he saw that, even lying down, April was doubled over, he told her to put her arms around his neck, and he scooped her up in his arms.

Downstairs, Elizabeth was on the phone in the den. "Do you want me to drive?" Paul asked.

"No," she answered, her hand over the mouthpiece. "Can you stay with Megan until Gladys comes?"

"Okay."

She hung up the phone, then hurried out the door behind him, grabbing coat and purse on the way.

Jesselene was waiting for them in the emergency room. Elizabeth had tried to calm April as they drove to the hospital, but her attempts had not been successful. April was still crying as the nurses brought out a wheelchair for her.

Both Jesselene and Elizabeth followed the wheelchair until it disappeared behind a curtain and a nurse directed them to the waiting room. They watched until Dr. Simmons waved to them and disappeared behind the curtain also. As they sat down on the vinyl sofa, Elizabeth turned to Jesselene beside her and sighed.

"She was almost hysterical," Jesselene said. "Is she in that much pain?"

"I think she's more afraid than anything else," Elizabeth said. Then a thought occurred to her. "Do you think she should call her mother?"

"Let's wait to hear what the doctor says, then I can call her. I brought the phone number with me."

About twenty minutes later, the nurses wheeled April by on a stretcher. She had calmed down and even managed a wan smile before she disappeared through the wide doors. Jesselene and Elizabeth stood uncertainly at the waiting-room door, unsure whether or not to follow the stretcher. But before they decided either way, Dr. Simmons walked from behind the curtain and came over to them.

"How is she?" Elizabeth asked.

"I'm not sure yet," he answered. "We've sent her to have a sonogram, so we'll know more after we see that. She hasn't lost the baby yet." He emphasized *yet*.

"Should we call her mother?" Jesselene asked.

"Yes. April should calm down more then. And her mother may have to sign a release form." He smiled at them both to reassure them. "We'll take care of her the best we can. And I'll talk to you after the sonogram."

April's mother was there within half an hour. Mrs. Hill

was a small nervous woman with the same sad eyes April had. She seemed relieved to have Jesselene and Elizabeth handling the situation. While the three women sat in the waiting room, Jesselene and Elizabeth told Mrs. Hill how much they had enjoyed getting to know April.

About twenty minutes later, Dr. Simmons came into the room. After being introduced to April's mother, he said, "We have determined what's wrong with April. The sonogram showed that the placenta is tearing loose, and there is quite a bit of bleeding."

"What can you do about it?" Jesselene asked.

"Not much," he said. "We're going to admit her to keep an eye on her. She hasn't lost the baby yet, but it's a real possibility. You can go see her in a minute."

"She won't want to see me," Mrs. Hill said. She looked as if she wanted to turn and run.

"Of course she does," Jesselene said. "You're her mother, and she loves you. She's just a frightened young girl trying to deal with grownup problems. She needs you." Jesselene tucked her arm into Mrs. Hill's arm and led her down the hall to the elevators.

Jesselene amazed Elizabeth. She had the ability to make everyone feel better, while Elizabeth stood there stumbling for the right thing to say. She wondered if that ability had come with age and experience, or if some people were just born naturally wonderful.

Jesselene was right. April was glad to see her mother and clung to her as Mrs. Hill leaned over the bed to hug her. "You'll be fine," her mother whispered to her. "You'll be fine."

"Thank you for coming, Mama," April said.

"I wouldn't be anyplace else." She let April go and stepped back for Jesselene and Elizabeth, who each hugged April and assured her that everything would be all right.

Obviously the medication April had been given was

beginning to make her drowsy, but Elizabeth wasn't sure whether she should offer to stay. She felt responsible for her since this had happened in her home. Still, her mother was there. Did her mother want to stay, though? "I'd be glad to stay with April if you'd like," she finally offered. "I can call my babysitter, and I know she would stay with my baby."

"No," her mother said. "I should be here. I can stay until my other children get home from school."

Elizabeth looked down to see what April's expression told her. She wanted her to feel as safe and secure as possible. But April looked happy about her mother staying, and Elizabeth again realized that there must be a place only a mother could fill.

"Can you come back tonight?" April asked Elizabeth. "When I got my tonsils taken out at the hospital, I got lonesome at night."

"I'd be glad to," Elizabeth said. "I'll stay as long as you like." She squeezed April's hand. "And I'll probably call you twenty times until then."

"If you need anything, you call me, too," Jesselene said.

"Okay," April replied. "Thank you."

Jesselene put her arm around Elizabeth as they walked down the hall. "It was good that her mother stayed with her," Jesselene said. "Wouldn't it be great if everything worked out between them?"

"I guess so," Elizabeth said hesitantly. "It sure would be lonesome around the house without her. We've gotten used to her being there."

Jesselene laughed softly. "You have empty nest syndrome before you've even survived the terrible twos and adolescence. I don't think you can do it in that order."

Elizabeth pushed the button when they reached the elevator and, on one of those unexplainable impulses, turned to Jesselene. "You're so . . . you're so good, Jesselene," she said. "You have this talent to make everyone feel better."

"Oh, thank you, dear," Jesselene said. "I'm just me."

"I know. But that is you. I could never be so good. I wouldn't know how to begin."

The elevator came, and they got on without comment. The elevator was empty so their conversation continued. "There was a time I was just as confused and lost as that girl in the hospital bed," Jesselene said. "But that was a lot of living and learning ago. The gospel came into my life, then Rowland, and since that time I've become a product of my religion and my family, I guess. It's no different than you could ever be, Elizabeth."

"I don't know. I couldn't dream of ever being the person you are."

"Oh, don't think that," she said with a kindly laugh. "You haven't seen me at my worst yet. You could be everything you like in me, plus be thinner and prettier."

After saying good-bye out in the parking lot, Elizabeth watched Jesselene walk down the rows of cars. Thinking about their conversation, she wondered at what point in her life Jesselene had been as lost as April was. She had always pictured Jesselene growing up with the same type of family life that she was giving her children. Would Jesselene have told her about it if they hadn't been on the elevator? If the time was right one day, maybe Elizabeth would ask her.

● ● ●

When Elizabeth got back to the hospital that evening, April's room was empty. The bed linens were rumpled, and the pitcher of ice water stood sweating on the nightstand, but there was no April. Before she could decide where the girl might be, a nurse came in with clean sheets.

"Is April okay?" Elizabeth asked. "I'm the woman she lives with."

"They took her down for an another sonogram a few minutes ago," the nurse said. "Her bleeding got worse."

"Oh no." Elizabeth sat down in the hard chair beside the window, fighting back tears. She felt so sorry for April having to deal with this after she had tried so hard to be brave and strong the last couple of weeks. As the nurse put the final tug on the top sheet, April was wheeled back in on the stretcher, Dr. Simmons walking beside it, holding her hand. He patted her arm, then walked over to Elizabeth.

"How is she?" Elizabeth asked. She stood up to meet him.

"It doesn't look good, Elizabeth. I can't believe she hasn't lost the baby yet, but she hasn't."

"Is there any hope she won't?"

"Well, a couple of times in the many years I've practiced, I've seen the placenta reattach itself, but it's very doubtful. I can't even explain why it's happened those times."

The nurses removed the stretcher, and April turned over and noticed Elizabeth. The doctor left, and Elizabeth pulled up the chair to sit closer to April. "So how are you feeling?" she asked.

"My stomach hurts a lot," April replied. "But they gave me something so it feels better. It makes me sleepy." She yawned.

"Just close your eyes then, and I'll sit here."

Her eyes had already closed as Elizabeth picked up a six-month-old copy of *Newsweek* from a little waiting table in the corner and thumbed through it.

"Elizabeth?" April asked quietly after a few minutes. Elizabeth had thought she was asleep.

"Yes, honey?" She closed the magazine and leaned over to hear better.

"Do you think God is punishing me for what I did?"

April was asking her a religious question? And expecting an answer? "Well . . . " She sat back a minute to think since she had never come to any solid conclusions about that matter in her life. But no, she didn't think he was. At least nothing she had learned from the Mormons indicated God would be punishing April. "No, of course, he isn't," Elizabeth said earnestly. "I'm sure he isn't punishing you. He loves you."

April seemed satisfied with the answer. And Elizabeth actually believed it herself, surprised that she had even said it. The God she had been reading about loved his children, even those who made mistakes.

"Do you think I'll lose the baby?" April asked next. Her eyes searched Elizabeth's face for some indication of hope to cling to.

Elizabeth mustered as much hope as she could. "I don't know, April, but everyone is doing everything they can to help you, so you get some rest, and maybe when you wake up, everything will be better."

"Okay." She smiled bravely, then shut her eyes again, snuggling down into her pillow. Her breathing became deep and even.

Elizabeth laid her arms up on the bed rails and leaned her forehead against them, her eyes aching with fatigue. It had seemed like such a long day, and suddenly her head hurt. She rested there, thinking only about the throbbing of her headache, until another thought burst through. She remembered a snatch of a conversation, one that she and Paul had had about the missionaries. Though she couldn't exactly recall which night it had occurred, the conversation came back to her with startling clarity. The missionaries had left for the hospital to administer to someone who was sick, to heal him or her, as Jesus had done in the Book of Mormon. Paul had explained it very briefly, but from her reading about the Savior's visit to the Nephites, she had come to understand something about priesthood and the Savior's power. She had dismissed the conversation then with only passing interest, but now, to her surprise, she believed it fervently. She could call the missionaries and ask them to come and heal April.

But, she wondered with a sinking feeling, would they come and do it to someone who wasn't a member of their church? They barely knew April or herself. About all they knew about Elizabeth Danforth was that she wasn't interested in anything they had to say.

But that wasn't true anymore. And Paul was a member of the Church now. He could ask them. Or Jesselene. Maybe she should call them instead. One thing was sure — whoever she asked was going to expect something of her now. The missionaries would know that she believed what they had been telling her, and Paul would beg her to be baptized. But really, wasn't it about time to bring her belief out into the open anyway?

All these thoughts raced around her head as she watched April sleep, occasionally groaning quietly, as if her body fought what was happening to her baby. Suddenly she realized her head no longer hurt, and in that same instant, she also knew that it didn't bother her who knew that she believed the gospel. She hadn't realized until now that her life had changed the moment she admitted that the Book of Mormon was true. And it wasn't frightening anymore. Her only fear was that she couldn't grab hold of it fast enough to help April.

For the first time in too many years for her to remember, she bowed her head against the bed railing and prayed. Please, please, she prayed. I'm sorry — I was wrong. Please, don't let it be too late. Please.

"April," she whispered. "I'll be back. Please, hang on. I'll be back." She didn't know if April heard her, but she hurried out of the room, a wonderful sense of lightness and peace filling her and melting the parts of her soul that had been so empty and cold for so long. Passing the people in the hall, she wondered if they could notice anything unusual about her, but they didn't seem to. To them, it was just a normal day, another shift to pull, another sick friend to visit. But as she walked out of the hospital and looked up at the darkening sunset, more beautiful than she had ever remembered it, she knew that this would never be just another day for her. This would always be the day that she had discovered and accepted faith. And for that, her heart overflowed with gratitude as she hurried to her car.

"Paul, Paul," she called from the front door several minutes later. "Where are you, Paul?"

"Up here in the baby's room," he answered.

He met her at the top of the stairs, worry across his face. "What's wrong?" he asked. "Is April okay?"

Noticing his look and realizing she must have scared him, she stopped to catch her breath and explain. "I didn't mean to scare you. April's okay. I mean, she's still not well, but I want you to help her."

"Me? What can I do?"

She pulled him down to sit on the step beside her. "Just listen to me and I'll explain. Do you remember when the missionaries came over and were going to the hospital to administer to someone who was sick?"

"Yes," he said. He looked thoroughly confused.

"I want you to get them to go and do it to April," she said. "I know it will make her better. Please. I don't want her to lose her baby."

"Do you know what you're saying, Bets? I didn't think you believed any of this."

"I didn't at first, honey." She put her hand on his arm and smiled at his astonishment. "I didn't tell you, but I've read the Book of Mormon and everything else you've left for me to read. I just can't fight it anymore. I know it's true and right, and I know what I want to do."

There were no words for him to say. He put his arms around her and held her until she pulled away.

"We can talk about this later, Paul. Please call the missionaries now before it's too late. I just know April will be all right."

He held her at arm's length, tears filling his eyes. "Okay, Bets, I will. And then we'll talk." Letting her go, he stood up, almost tripping over Megan, who had crawled up behind him. He picked her up and planted a big kiss on her neck before he swung her over to Elizabeth.

Elizabeth hugged Megan, burying her face in her sweet softness, as she listened to Paul dial the phone. She knew they would talk later; there was so much to say, so much to learn. Maybe even enough to fill an eternity together. But first there was still April, and Elizabeth bowed her head and prayed again.

● ● ●

Elizabeth didn't have to do much talking to convince April to let the missionaries come to administer to her. Though Elizabeth didn't understand exactly what the missionaries did during the blessing, her intensity and April's fear for her baby's life made it a quick decision. "I'll do anything you say, Elizabeth," April said, "anything."

The missionaries arrived almost immediately, but if they were surprised by the enthusiasm Elizabeth showed at their arrival, they hid it well. Elizabeth stood beside the bed, holding tightly onto April's hand, and wondered what she was supposed to do while this went on. April closed her eyes as Elder Thorne uncapped a bottle of oil, but out of curiosity, Elizabeth watched as he poured a tiny amount on April's head and said a prayer. She closed her eyes then and offered her own pleading, as Elder Harrison spoke April's name and said another prayer.

In his prayer, he blessed April that her baby's life would be spared and that she would have the wisdom and strength she needed to make decisions about her life. He spoke so deliberately and eloquently that Elizabeth peeped to see if Elder Harrison was the one still speaking.

When it was over, April had tears on her cheeks, and Elizabeth could barely manage a "thank you" because of the thickness in her throat. "I know I'll be okay," April told the missionaries. "I could feel something inside when you prayed. Did you feel it too, Elizabeth?"

"Yes, I did," Elizabeth said, patting April's hand. She had felt something—like a spark, or a strength, passing through April's body as Elizabeth had held her hand. She didn't know how she knew, but she knew for sure that April and her baby would be all right.

22

April came home from the hospital two days later on a Sunday afternoon. Dr. Simmons was still shaking his head over her recovery when he signed her out. "You're a lucky young lady," he kept saying. "A lucky young lady."

Paul met April and Elizabeth at the door, with Megan in his arms. "Hey, April," he said, "are you feeling okay?"

"Just fine," she answered with a smile. "Thanks for letting me come back here. And thank you for bringing the missionaries. It saved my baby."

"You're welcome, and you can stay here as long as you need and want to," he said. Handing Megan over to Elizabeth, he slipped past them through the door. "I'll go get the bags."

Elizabeth fussed over April, helping her inside the house. "Do you need to lie down?"

"No, I'm fine," she said. "Can I just sit in the den for a little while?"

"Sure. I'll go fix some lunch."

When Paul returned to the kitchen, he came up behind

Elizabeth and grabbed her around the waist. "You're in a good mood," he said.

"Sure am," she answered. "Here, spread some mayonnaise." She handed him a knife. "I've been happy the last couple of days, or haven't you noticed?"

"I've noticed. So, are the missionaries coming tonight?"

"At seven. They said I could probably finish the discussions this week and be baptized next Sunday." She opened the cupboard to pull out some chips. "Here, put these on the table."

"You're sure you want to be baptized so soon?" he asked, putting down the knife and picking up the bag.

"Don't you want me to?"

"You know I do. It's just such a sudden departure from the way you've always been."

"It didn't happen overnight, Paul. I just didn't tell you about it." She put the sandwiches down and looked at him intently. "It took me a while to decide I wanted to change my outlook." They had talked a lot about her feelings for the gospel since she had told him that she wanted to join the Church. "I'm sure that I can finally stop hoping to find my mother one day. I'm not sure I understand the reason for the way I grew up, but I think there was a reason for it. There must be some reason I don't know about yet that explains why I haven't been able to find my mother."

"She could be dead, you know," Paul said gently. "You've never wanted to accept that possibility before."

"I know, and maybe I still don't. But I'm going to put that part of my life to rest and start all over again with you and Megan and any other children we might have. I've found a greater purpose in life than finding my past, and I'm going to start looking forward, not backward."

Paul leaned over and, taking her face in both his hands, kissed her gently on her cheek. "I love you, Bets. You don't know how happy you make me." He kissed her again on the lips.

"Yes, I do," she said, "because you make me twice as happy." She took his hands from her face and held them between her hands.

They were sitting at the table, sandwiches and potato chips untouched, looking happily at each other, when April walked into the kitchen, carrying Megan. "Can we help with anything?" April asked. "Megan says we're hungry."

Elizabeth jumped up, laughing, and grabbed Megan, lifting her up. "Come on, then, Megan. We'll feed you and your hungry friend here." She put an arm around April for a quick squeeze. "We're so happy you're all right, April."

● ● ●

Every morning that week, Elizabeth had awakened wondering what would happen that day to spoil the happiness and peace she'd felt since she had told Paul of her decision to join the Church. But it was finally Sunday afternoon and nothing had happened to spoil anything; the week was one of the happiest she could remember. Everything she had learned as the missionaries taught her that week put her life into a breathtaking perspective. After so many years, she was finally free from her past. It was also wonderful to be able to share it with Paul, not having to keep any part of her life locked up from him anymore.

Right now though, she was trying to be cool and collected, but she had already tried on four different outfits. What was the perfect dress to wear to your baptism anyway? Looking in the mirror, she decided it certainly wasn't what she had on and started to unzip it in the back.

"Here, let me help," Paul said. He zipped it right back up.

"What are you doing?" she asked. "I look fat in this."

"You do not. You look perfect, and it's time to go."

"Are you sure?" she asked.

"On both counts." He handed her purse to her. "Let's go."

"Wait," she said, turning back. "I want to wear my baby ring necklace today." She took it gently from its drawer and looked at it, holding it up against the light. "I've thought about it all week and decided that I've worn it at every big moment of my life, so I want to wear it at my baptism. Now help me put it on quick so we can go. It's getting late."

"I've been saying that," he said, fastening her necklace.

About twenty minutes later, they were sitting in the baptismal service. Two little boys, Shawn and Daniel, were being baptized also, and Elizabeth kept thinking that they looked perfectly calm as they sat beside their fathers, dressed in white. Elizabeth was sitting between Nephi, who was going to baptize her, and Paul, whom she wouldn't let leave her side. Jesselene had Megan a couple of rows back.

"They look so excited," Elizabeth said to Paul about the little boys.

"They've had eight years to look forward to this," he whispered back.

"I'm so nervous." She showed him her shaking hands.

"You'll be fine." He took her hands from her lap and held them firmly in his own.

While Jeanine held Megan, Jesselene gave a short talk about baptism that gave Elizabeth goose bumps at the thought of the importance of what she was doing. But as she finished, and Shawn was baptized, the goose bumps faded, and a wonderful warmth that Elizabeth had learned to recognize replaced them. As Daniel came up out of the font, she took her hand from Paul, took a deep breath, and walked to the top step of the stairway leading into the water.

She watched Nephi descend into the font, reach the middle, then motion her to follow him.

Although, to her surprise, the water was warm, she trembled with anticipation as she walked down to meet Nephi. She could hear Megan babbling and glanced up to catch Paul's smile of reassurance before she took Nephi's hand.

It was over before she could grab the moment and savor it. Wiping the water from her eyes, she smiled up at Nephi and took his hand as he helped her up the stairs. From the corner of her eye, she saw Jesselene hand Megan over to Paul and head for the side door. She had promised Elizabeth that she would meet her in the bathroom after her baptism and help with her wet clothes.

As she started up the stairs, her wet dress clinging to her, she looked over at Paul and smiled. He hadn't cried at his own baptism, but she could see tears on his cheeks. He looked a little embarrassed and picked up Megan's hand and waved it at Elizabeth.

Whether from the coolness of the bathroom or from excitement, Elizabeth shivered as she toweled off her hair and wrung the water from the hem of her dress. Jesselene came in the bathroom and knocked on the door to the dressing stall.

"Elizabeth," she said excitedly. "It was beautiful. How do you feel?"

"Wonderful!" Elizabeth exclaimed. "I wish I could feel this way forever."

"Well," Jesselene said. "I don't know how possible that is, but you can try." She and Elizabeth laughed. "Here, hand your wet clothes over, and I'll wring them out and hang them up."

She and Jesselene talked through the door as Elizabeth dressed. Before putting on her dress, she suddenly remembered her necklace. Afraid that she might lose it somehow in the font, she had removed it, wrapped it in a tissue, and placed it in her purse before her baptism. Now she carefully took it out, unwrapped it, and started to put it around her neck.

"Oh no!" she said. The clasp to the chain came loose, and the tiny ring fell off and rolled across the floor past the drain to disappear under the stall door.

"What's wrong, dear?" Jesselene asked.

"I dropped the ring that goes on my necklace," she said. "It rolled under the door. Do you see it? It's a tiny little baby ring."

"I see it," Jesselene said. "What a pretty little ring."

Elizabeth put on her dress, but there was no sound from the other side of the door. "Are you still there?" Elizabeth asked.

"Yes," Jesselene answered after a pause. Then, in a whisper Elizabeth almost didn't catch, Jesselene asked, "Where did you get the baby ring?"

"It was my mother's," she said. She picked up her brush and hair dryer and opened the door. Jesselene jumped from where she had been leaning against the wall. She looked awfully pale to Elizabeth.

"Are these initials your mother's?" she asked quietly.

"Yes," Elizabeth said. "Are you all right? You look aw-fully pale." She took the ring that Jesselene held out to her.

"I'm . . . fine," Jesselene said. "I just have a terrible headache. That's all." She massaged her temples. "Your mother—did you know her? I mean, you said your parents were killed when you were young."

Elizabeth smiled apologetically. It wouldn't hurt to tell Jesselene now. It didn't matter as much. "Those were my adoptive parents. My real mother gave me up for adoption. This is all I have of hers."

"Oh," Jesselene said. She smiled weakly.

"Maybe you should go sit down, Jesselene," Elizabeth urged. "You look so pale. I'll just dry my hair a little."

"Okay." She looked at Elizabeth as if she wanted to say something more, but instead pursed her lips tightly. She started to move slowly toward the door. Elizabeth reached out to help her, but Jesselene held her hand up. "I'm fine," she said. "Just a terrible headache."

Elizabeth replaced the ring on the chain and put it around her neck. Hurrying because it seemed that she had spent so much time in the dressing room already, she plugged in the dryer and began quickly drying her hair. Smiling at herself in the mirror, she caught sight of the little ring around her neck and thought back to the lonely little girl who used to finger it on its string every night. Those days seemed so far removed from the joy she felt now.

But she did hope Jesselene would feel better. It must have been a terrible headache to come on so suddenly and make her so pale. She shook her head and left the dressing room.

Paul was out in the hall trying to quiet a fussy Megan. He handed her over to Elizabeth with relief. "She didn't know where her mommy was," he said.

Megan threw herself into Elizabeth's arms. "Did you see Jesselene?" she asked. "She said she had a terrible headache and left."

"She went home?" he asked.

"I don't know. I don't see her anywhere, but Rowland is sitting right over there." Through the door, she indicated a spot about four rows from the front. "Maybe we should ask him."

"We'll find out as soon as you're confirmed." He patted her shoulder reassuringly. "I think they're waiting for you."

"I hope she'll be all right." He didn't seem too worried, but he hadn't seen how pale she had been. They went back into the room and sat down.

Jeanine gave the talk about the Holy Ghost. Elizabeth listened attentively and gradually relaxed. It wasn't hard to do because, after Paul had told her about the experience of his confirmation, she had been excited. In fact, she hadn't felt this much excitement and joy since Megan had been born. She wondered if all joy came from the same source. It really was an almost perfect day. If only she knew that Jesselene was okay, it could be.

Barely turning in her seat, she could see Rowland a couple of rows back, but he didn't seem concerned about where Jesselene was. She turned back to where Shawn was being seated in a chair up front. Soon she would be receiving the same wonderful gift.

●   ●   ●

Jesselene finally made it outside the church, where she stopped and leaned against the wall, her face in her hands. She didn't know what to feel inside, though her legs felt like jelly now that she had stopped walking, and her throat had closed up so tightly that she was suffocating. After all these years of praying and thinking about her daughter, she had given up, only to find her so close that she could touch her. Tears filled her eyes and spilled over, burning her cheeks, but she didn't know if they were tears of happiness or . . . guilt.

All she knew was that she had to get away before anyone came out because she couldn't talk. She could barely even breathe. She concentrated on making her legs move, one in front of the other, until she reached the cars. Her hands shook so badly it took several tries to start the car.

She didn't even remember the trip home, but by the time she reached her bedroom and locked the door behind her, even though no one was home, she could almost breathe normally again. Laying her purse and keys down, she took off her coat and walked over to the dresser to look at herself. She was frightfully pale. She dabbed her eyes with a tissue and caught sight of the picture of her children on the dresser. As she picked it up and stared at Diane, it all made sense—the remarkable resemblance between Elizabeth and Diane and between Diane's baby pictures and Megan. She had felt so close to Elizabeth from the beginning, a kinship she had really not questioned.

She put down the picture and went over to curl up on the bed. Was Elizabeth ready for a mother? Elizabeth had told her after she decided to be baptized that she had finally decided to close the book on her unhappy childhood and stop dwelling on it.

Her unhappy childhood. What had Elizabeth told her about her adoptive parents—that they had been killed in a car accident? So she had spent her childhood with no real family. That thought started Jesselene's tears anew. All those years she had consoled herself with the fact that a loving couple had adopted her daughter. But none of it had happened.

How would Elizabeth feel about her if Elizabeth knew that Jesselene was her mother? Elizabeth had never said that she hated her mother for giving her up, but she had felt abandoned and cheated, so she must blame her mother to some extent. She had even blamed God for years.

Jesselene's thoughts raced around and around until her mind was numb trying to figure out what to do. She had read so many magazine stories about mothers and children being reunited years after being separated, but now she couldn't remember a single ending. Perhaps she wouldn't say anything to Elizabeth. But then, how could she keep it secret? Her head ached with the possibilities.

She was still lying on the bed when someone rattled the doorknob and knocked. "Jesselene?" Rowland called. "Jess? Why is the door locked? Are you all right?"

She hadn't even heard her family come home. She didn't want to see or talk to anyone, but she owed Rowland some kind of an explanation. Yet she couldn't, she just couldn't, tell him yet. If she put it in words, she'd have to face the situation and make some decision about it, and she wasn't ready to do that.

Dabbing quickly at her eyes, she walked over and opened the door. When she saw Rowland, her throat choked with tears again. She turned, hoping he wouldn't see her face, and went to sit on the edge of the bed, but he walked right over and put his hand on her shoulder. "Are you all right, honey?" he asked. "Elizabeth said you got sick and left. Why didn't you get me?"

"I'm okay," she said with difficulty. "I just need to rest a little. Dinner's in the oven."

Rowland came around and sat on the other side of her where he could see her face. She covered her eyes with a tissue, but he pulled her hands down. "Jesselene, what's wrong? You look like you've been crying for hours."

She tried but couldn't speak. All she could do was collapse in tears against him as he held her.

"What's wrong with Mom?" Steve asked from the doorway. "Is she all right?"

"I don't know yet," Rowland said. "Why don't you and Diane go get some dinner? It's in the oven."

Steve stood at the door until Rowland said firmly, "Go, Steve." Reluctantly he left and shut the door behind him.

Rowland held her until Jesselene was too tired to sob anymore. He went into the bathroom and brought her a glass of water, standing before her until she drank it. She didn't look up at him but said, "You must be hungry. Why don't you go eat with the kids?"

"I'll eat when I know what's wrong with you." He pulled his tie off and carefully folded his coat over the chair before sitting down beside her. "What happened at church to upset you so much? Was it something to do with the baptism?"

"I just don't think I can talk about it," she said.

"Of course you can," he said. "I can't imagine what could have happened at church that you couldn't talk about. It can't be that bad."

"It is." She felt that she needed to tell him — he would tell her what to do.

"Tell me then," he insisted. "I can help you with it."

She looked him straight in the eye. "Elizabeth is my daughter," she said.

"Your daughter? What do you mean?"

"My daughter I gave up for adoption. It's Elizabeth."

He was still puzzled. "What makes you think that?"

"I never told you, Rowland. I don't know why, but I didn't tell you that I sent my baby ring with my baby. And Elizabeth has it. She has my ring."

Rowland paused for a long time, then breathed deeply. "Did you see it?"

"She dropped it in the dressing room. I saw it. She said it was her mother's."

"Maybe it's not the same ring," he said hopefully.

"My initials are in it, honey."

Again, Rowland was silent.

Jesselene continued when Rowland didn't say anything. "I'm sure she's my daughter. Don't you see? That's why she and Diane look so much alike."

"Oh" was all he said, putting his arm around her. His expression was puzzled. "But why are so upset, honey? You've wondered for so many years, I'd think you'd be more happy than sad. You've found another beautiful daughter."

Jesselene stood up and went to lean against the window before she answered. "What if she doesn't want a mother? What if she blames me for giving her up? She never had a real family, Rowland. Her adoptive parents were killed just a few months after her adoption."

"I'm sure she's wanted to find her mother. It's only natural."

"But our children don't know anything about this. What will they think? They'll be so ashamed."

"Give our children some credit, Jesselene. They love you, and they know you."

"So much time has passed, Rowland. It might be best to never mention it. She was so happy after her baptism. This might change things. It might change her whole attitude about the Church, finding out I gave her away."

"I don't think so," he said gently. "It might not be easy, but I'm sure we can work through any problems." He came to stand behind her and put his arms around her. "I'm sure if you think and pray about it, you'll know what to do. And Elizabeth already loves you. I think she'd be thrilled to know you're her mother."

"Really?" Jesselene was so relieved that she had told him. The more he talked, the more hopeful she became that Elizabeth's reaction would be a positive one. Still, how could she know for sure? Did she want to be responsible for causing her even more pain? She turned to slip her arms around Rowland. "Thank you, dear. I need to do some serious thinking and praying. Why don't you go eat dinner and let me be alone for a while?"

"I guess so, but I'll bring you up some dinner in a little bit. Okay?"

"Okay." She gave him one last hug. "I love you," she said.

"I love you too."

But before he could get to the door, she called him again. "Rowland, what will you tell the kids?"

"Beats me," he said, smiling.

23

Elizabeth had called the Mannings that evening after she and Paul had put Megan to bed. Rowland had answered and said that Jesselene was feeling better but was still up in her room. He assured her that Jesselene would call her when she felt better. Elizabeth had worried about her since she'd left church—Jesselene had looked so pale and shaky. She wondered if Rowland had taken Jesselene to the doctor yet.

In case Jesselene was still not feeling well, she waited until Monday afternoon when Steve came home from school. She then asked April to watch Megan a minute while she made the phone call.

Steve did answer.

"Hi, Steve," she said. "This is Elizabeth. Is your mother feeling any better today?"

"Oh, hi, Elizabeth," he said. "I just got home from school, so I haven't seen her yet. Let me go see if I can find her. Hang on."

Elizabeth waited, hoping that Jesselene would be on the phone next, but she soon heard a male voice again.

"Elizabeth?" Steve asked.

"Yes."

"She said to tell you that she's feeling better but not well enough to come to the phone. She said she plans on calling you in the morning if that's okay."

"That will be great," Elizabeth said. "I've been worried about her ever since she left church Sunday. Has she had a virus or something?"

"Beats me," Steve said. "I've hardly seen her, and Dad told us to leave her alone." He whispered into the phone conspiratorially. "She was crying a lot yesterday."

"Crying?" Elizabeth asked. "Why?"

"I don't know."

"Hmmm." Elizabeth didn't want to pry too much. "Thanks, Steve. Will you tell your mother that I'll look forward to her call in the morning?"

"Sure thing," he said.

Why would Jesselene be crying a lot after she left her baptism? Elizabeth sat in her bedroom and wondered, thinking back to what had happened that day, but she couldn't think of anything that would have upset her so much. She couldn't remember saying anything that would have made her mad or hurt her feelings. Maybe after she'd left church with a headache, something else had happened. She finally shrugged to herself and replaced the phone on the hook. She'd just have to wait till morning.

• • •

Jesselene did call the next morning, but she still didn't explain. Elizabeth had stayed home waiting for her call, which hadn't come until almost ten o'clock.

"Hi," Elizabeth said, after hearing her voice. "It's so good to talk to you. I've been worried about you."

Jesselene laughed — a short, nervous laugh, Elizabeth thought. "That's sweet of you," Jesselene said.

"Have you been sick? I couldn't figure out what had happened to you at church."

"Well, sort of," Jesselene answered. There was a silence between them, just long enough to get uncomfortable, then Jesselene spoke again. "I can't go into it over the phone, Elizabeth, but I called to see if Rowland and I could come over this evening and see you and Paul. Will he be home?"

"He said he'd be home about six." Elizabeth was really puzzled now. She had to ask. "Have I done anything to make you mad?"

"Oh no, honey," Jesselene assured her. "You could never make me mad."

Elizabeth wasn't sure, but it sounded as if Jesselene were beginning to cry. But why?

"Can we come over?" she asked again, sniffling. "I'll explain everything then."

"Sure," Elizabeth said. "We'll be here all evening. Come anytime you want."

Jesselene mumbled a quick thanks and hung up. Elizabeth stared at the phone again, wondering what was so mysterious or important that Rowland and Jesselene needed to come over to explain it. She sighed. She was getting used to waiting for answers.

● ● ●

The Mannings had pulled into the driveway at seven fourteen, but they still weren't out of the car at seven nineteen. "What do you think they're waiting for?" Elizabeth asked Paul. She peeked out of the drape again.

Paul was reading the newspaper. "I don't know, sweetheart. Why don't you go ask them?"

"You can't blame me for being nervous. She sounded as if I had done something to upset her."

"But she said you hadn't." He folded the paper and laid it beside his chair.

"Then why are they coming over?" Paul must be getting tired of that question, she thought to herself. "Wait— they're getting out." She pulled the drape back into place and quickly sat down on the couch.

Paul laughed.

"Well, I don't want them to think I know they've been here for five minutes already."

The doorbell rang. "I'll get it," Paul said.

As Paul walked toward the door, Elizabeth followed right behind. He opened the door, and she peered over his shoulder. Rowland was smiling slightly, and his arm was tightly around Jesselene, who looked just as pale as she had on Sunday.

"Hi, come on in," Paul said.

Rowland and Paul exchanged a few words about the weather, but Elizabeth said nothing as they walked into the den. Maybe she should have asked if Jesselene was feeling better since she was still so pale, but not knowing exactly what had caused her paleness, she was afraid to say anything. Jesselene sat down on the couch, but Rowland continued to stand at the end of it. Elizabeth sat down beside her, while Paul stood awkwardly waiting for Rowland to sit down.

Jesselene looked at Elizabeth, then up at Rowland. Rowland looked at Jesselene, then over at Paul. Rubbing his hands together, he said, "Could we go someplace and leave the ladies alone for a little while, Paul?"

Paul and Elizabeth looked at each other, even more puzzled now, but Paul recovered quickly. "Of course," he said. "We can go out in the kitchen."

When they left, Jesselene smiled at Elizabeth weakly. They were sitting close enough for Jesselene to take Elizabeth's hand, but she touched her hand only briefly, then drew hers back onto her lap.

Elizabeth could stand it no longer. "What's wrong, Jesselene? Have I done something to upset you?"

"No, dear," she said. She took Elizabeth's hand then and looked into her eyes. "I have something very difficult to tell you, and I'm not sure how you're going to take it. I've grown to love you and your family, and I don't want to lose you."

"You won't lose us," Elizabeth assured her. "I just can't imagine what it is. Please just tell me and don't worry."

"Okay," she said. "I'll try to find the words. After another long pause, she sighed and began. "When I was fifteen, I wasn't a member of the Church, any church for that matter, and I fell in love, or so I thought, with a boy a couple of years older. We got involved pretty seriously, and before I really understood what had happened, I found myself pregnant."

"Now I understand," Elizabeth said, almost to herself.

"You do?" Jesselene asked.

"Now I understand your tremendous empathy with the girls we help." That was clear, but what was it leading to?

"Oh," Jesselene said. "I guess so."

"I'm sorry. Go on," Elizabeth said kindly. Jesselene was having enough trouble with the story without her interruptions.

"My parents, of course, were upset. My father especially was angry and insisted that I give up the baby for adoption. Thank goodness, abortions were illegal then, or he might have insisted on that." She shook her head at the thought. "I was young and scared, and I knew I couldn't give a baby a good life."

"I can understand that," Elizabeth assured her. It was hard to sit and listen to her good friend talk through such obvious pain.

"I stayed with an aunt in another town until my baby was born, then my father came with a social worker, and they assured me that they had found a wonderful couple who could give my baby a lot of love." Jesselene suddenly squeezed Elizabeth's hands and spoke with intensity. "Please, believe me, Elizabeth. I know they were telling me the truth. I just didn't know how it would turn out. All these years as I've wondered about my baby girl, my only comfort has been that I knew she was with a kind and loving family. Please believe me."

"I do," Elizabeth said. Her whole body was beginning to tingle, every nerve she had standing on edge. This story was beginning to sound familiar.

"I saw my baby before she left, only once, but I sent the only thing I could give her, and my father promised me that it would go with her." She looked down at her hands and closed her eyes, as if praying for strength to go on. "It was my baby ring."

Elizabeth's hand automatically flew to her throat even though she had put her necklace away after the baptism. She drew in her breath sharply.

"I sent my ring with her, with my initials on it. My first name is Karen. My maiden name is Lassiter. My parents always called me Jesselene, though — after my grandmother. Jesselene's my middle name." She lifted her eyes up to Elizabeth, who was staring wide-eyed at her.

Elizabeth gasped, not believing what she had heard but expecting the next sentence.

"Elizabeth," Jesselene said, "you are my daughter."

"Your daughter?" Her throat tightened. "Are you sure?"

"Yes." She searched Elizabeth's face. "I'm so sorry."

Elizabeth didn't understand through the fog in her mind. "You're sorry I'm your . . . your daughter."

"No, that I'm thrilled about. I loved you already as a daughter. I'm so sorry about the couple who was killed before you even knew them, and I'm so sorry for the loneliness and pain you grew up with."

"I always thought my mother didn't love me, didn't want me."

"I did. Oh, I did love you. But I was so young and so scared. Can you understand that?"

A few weeks ago, Elizabeth wouldn't have understood, but now, as she thought of April and the other scared young girls she had met the last few weeks, she had to admit that she could understand. "I can," she said. "Now I can."

"There was never a day, hardly a minute that I haven't thought about you, wondering where you were and what you were doing. But I gave up long ago hoping that I would ever find you."

"My ring," Elizabeth whispered. "You saw my ring." Her mind was beginning to thaw, full of questions, wanting to be sure before she gave the woman before her what she wanted so much to give.

"At your baptism . . . when you dropped your ring and I picked it up. When I held it in my hand, it was as if I had never let it go, had never put it on your finger."

"K. L.," Elizabeth whispered. "Karen Lassiter."

Jesselene smiled hesitantly.

"You are my mother," Elizabeth breathed, believing her fully.

Jesselene nodded. Her eyes filled with tears. "I love you, Elizabeth, but if you never want to see me again and can't forgive me, or if it will take a long time, I'll wait, or I'll leave now and you'll never see me again."

Elizabeth started to speak, but her throat choked with tears. "I've waited for so many years to find my mother. It almost kept me from being baptized." Tears spilled over at that thought. "Jesselene, I never in all my dreams imagined my mother to be as good and kind as you are. How could I let you leave and never see you again after wanting you for so long? Believe me—I love you dearly." She took Jesselene in her arms, both of them crying now. "I've found you. After all these years, I've found you."

"I'll make it up to you, Elizabeth," Jesselene cried. "I promise I will."

"You already have, Jesselene. You've given me the gospel and the Church." Something suddenly occurred to her, and she sat up straight, releasing Jesselene. "I have a brother and sister!" she exclaimed. She grabbed Jesselene again. "It's wonderful. It's wonderful."

A little later, the men came back into the room to find their wives, mother and daughter, alternately laughing and crying. Tears were on Paul's cheeks. Evidently Rowland had told him. He hugged Elizabeth, then Jesselene. "I'm so happy for you both," he said. "Our long search has ended."

"Can you bring Diane and Steve over? Do they know?" Elizabeth asked. She was anxious to get everyone together before she missed another minute or second.

"Not yet," Rowland said. "It will be a shock for them, but I know they'll be thrilled to have a sister like you."

It was so much to take in and understand that Elizabeth felt as if she would burst. She had dreamed about this moment all of her life, yet she had never pictured it this way. She had thought that she would be the one to walk up to the door of the woman she had discovered. Or she'd receive a mysterious letter in the mail from a woman she didn't know. But now, not only had her mother found her, but she was also one of her dearest friends.

Rowland and Jesselene stayed late into the night, until finally at midnight Steve called to see if they were still there. "We'll be home soon," Jesselene assured him. "Go on to bed."

"I guess we'd better leave," she told Elizabeth. They had spent the last few hours sharing their lives with each other, asking and answering a hundred questions.

"Oh, I don't want you to go," Elizabeth said. "I'm afraid I'll never see you again. I just found you." She put her arms around Jesselene once more.

"You'll see me again. In fact, you'll see me so much that you'll get sick of me. I have a granddaughter to get to know and spoil."

"When will you tell Diane and Steve?" Elizabeth asked.

Jesselene looked at Rowland. "Probably tomorrow afternoon. I'll have to think about how to do it."

"I'll be patient. I promise."

Jesselene touched Elizabeth's cheek. "What a blessing," she said. "What a wonderful blessing has come to me."

"No," Elizabeth said, tears flowing once again. "The blessing is mine."

Epilogue

A year later, on the date she had been baptized, Paul and Elizabeth drove with Megan into the Washington Temple parking lot. They got out as a station wagon and a van pulled up next to them. Rowland, Jesselene, Diane, and Steve climbed out from the wagon, while Nephi and Jeanine got out from the van. Megan toddled over to her grandmother.

Two hours later, Paul and Elizabeth walked into a temple sealing room with Rowland, Jesselene, Nephi, and Jeanine. The beauty of the mirrors took Elizabeth's breath away. She turned to Paul, squeezing his hand with both of hers. "It's beautiful," she said in a whisper.

"Everything today is beautiful," he whispered back. He kissed the top of her head. "Especially you."

A few minutes later, they knelt across the altar from each other and were sealed for time and eternity. A temple worker appeared silently with Megan in her arms, looking like a tiny angel in her white gown. She handed her to Jesselene, who knelt down and held her little granddaughter as Megan was sealed to Paul and Elizabeth. Afterwards, still wide-eyed and miraculously quiet, Megan disappeared with the temple worker again.

Elizabeth turned to Jesselene, joy on her face. She embraced her and whispered into her ear, "This is the happiest day of my life."

"Mine, too," Jesselene answered.

Then around the altar, Rowland, Jesselene, and Elizabeth knelt, hands clasped, as they were sealed together. Elizabeth thought her heart would burst with happiness.

It had been a wonderful year with a new family, but at that moment around the altar, she knew that it had just begun. At last, and forever, like the baby ring hanging at her neck, her past and future had merged with the present into a perfect continuous round, encircling her with a happiness fuller and more vast than she had ever dreamed could exist.